DRUG ADDICTION

DRUG ADDICTION

"NO WAY I'M NOT AN ADDICT"

JOHN HICKS

THE MILLBROOK PRESS   BROOKFIELD, CONNECTICUT

Library of Congress Cataloging-in-Publication Data
Hicks, John, 1951–
Drug addiction: no way I'm an addict / John Hicks.
p. cm.
Includes bibliographical references and index.
Summary: Informational text and first-person
narratives demonstrate the development of drug
addiction, the nature of the addiction, and the
possibilities of recovery.
ISBN 0-7613-0202-6 (lib. bdg.)
1. Teenagers—Drug use—United States—Juvenile
literature. 2. Drug abuse—United States—Prevention—Juvenile literature. [1. Drug abuse. 2. Drugs.]
I. Title.
HV5824.Y68H53   1997
613.8—dc21   97-1105   CIP   AC

Published by The Millbrook Press, Inc.
2 Old New Milford Road
Brookfield, Connecticut 06804

Contents

DRUG ADDICTION

WHY ANOTHER BOOK ABOUT DRUG ADDICTION?

For the last six years, I have been on call at the emergency room of a local hospital. Late at night or on weekends, I meet with people who have come in crisis, or who want help with an addictive illness. Often, they have just narrowly escaped death through an accidental overdose. Many are accompanied by police, having threatened or attempted suicide. Some are just sick and tired of being sick and tired. But all are desperate to get out of their daily routine of being strung out and scrambling for the drink or drug to delay withdrawal. For these people there is no "high" in getting high from drugs or alcohol; there is just avoiding the reality that their lives amount to only this meaningless cycle.

Almost without exception, all of these people began drinking or using drugs while they were in their teens. A few are still teenagers, usually those who have been brought in by a rescue squad following an accidental overdose or suicide attempt. But the vast majority of those seeking treatment, young and old, became addicted during high school or soon after. Even the exceptions to this rule, those who developed a serious addiction in their thirties or forties, began their use of mood-altering substances while still in their teens. For these people as well, the road to addiction began during high school—it just took longer to get there.

The fact that most addicts begin when in high school, or even younger, is not startling news when you consider the number of high school and junior high school students who are currently using drugs and alcohol. A 1993 study by the Illinois Drug Education Alliance compiled statistics showing that 37 percent of high school students had used pot, that during the previous month 43 percent of tenth graders had used alcohol, and that 13 percent of eighth graders reported a drinking binge of five or more drinks at one sitting. The *Monitoring the Future* survey of high school students conducted since 1975 by the Institute for Social Research at the University of Michigan reported in December 1996 that students using pot in that year included 36 percent of twelfth graders, 34 percent of tenth graders, and 18 percent of eighth graders. This was three times the number of eighth graders who reported smoking pot in 1991. The survey showed an increase over the previous three years in all grades for other drugs as well, including cocaine, LSD and other hallucinogens, heroin, stimulants, and barbiturates.

Although these figures are alarmingly high, most young people of high school age choose to abstain from drugs entirely. Abstinence is a sure way to avoid addiction, and it has an important place both in the prevention of drug abuse and in the recovery from addiction. But once someone has chosen to experiment with an addictive substance, it's too late to "Just Say No." This growing number of young people who have tried substances are caught somewhere between abstinence and addiction, and they may have little information about what choices to make now or where those choices will lead.

Young people are themselves concerned about the rise of drug use. According to the *New York Times* of July 18, 1995, 32 percent of the high school students surveyed by the Center on Addiction and Substance Abuse at Columbia University believed that drugs were the "biggest problem they face, far outranking crime, social pressure, grades, or sex." And 30 percent "thought that it was easy to get cocaine and heroin." The *New York Times* went on to report that "adults and adolescents alike believed that smoking cigarettes or drinking alcohol was the first step toward illegal drug use."

At the point where the people I see come in for help, they have been using addictive substances on and off for five, ten, maybe twenty years. Our work together involves identifying the problem and helping them engage with the resources they'll need to begin healing. They then enter the difficult, often unsuccessful process of treatment. Once chronic chemical dependence has taken hold, it may take many attempts before treatment is successful. Those who manage to get clean and sober still have to deal with the damage that years of addictive behavior have done to their lives—and the lives of those around them. They are forced to look back at how much has been lost: the dreams and hopes they once had for the future, friends and family who are alienated and hurt, the cumulative abuse and neglect of their bodies, the wasted years and missed opportunities that can never be replaced, the toll on their emotional and spiritual health.

Faced with this reality week after week, year after year, I wondered if something could have been done sooner. Was there something that could have been said before these young people started down this road that might have driven them to make different choices? What information might have helped predict the consequences of their drug use? I thought back to my own teenage drug abuse, the poor choices I made under the influence of alcohol and hallucinogens, and how they have affected my life ever since. Was there something to be learned from all this loss and unhappiness, both in my own life and the lives of the addicts I have worked with, that could give these losses some meaning?

This book is an attempt to answer these questions. In it you will be introduced to young people who have known firsthand the soul-killing power of addiction. Their names and identifying details have been changed to protect their confidentiality, but their stories are real. These young people share feelings and beliefs about the substances they have used, and they communicate a sense of what they were hoping to gain by first picking up a drink or a drug. Each one doubted that he or she could ever become an addict. For readers who are thinking about trying drugs, the stories will serve as examples of what they can expect, and may convince them that using alcohol, tobacco, or other drugs is not what their friends or the advertising media promise it will be. For those who are experiencing some confusion about their current drug use or who are having problems in other areas of their lives, these stories should help them become aware of how substance abuse affects the lives of young people, and can help them to make better choices about what to do now. Accurate information about addiction is a valuable tool for people of any age in learning about their relationship to substances and what the dangers are.

Perhaps a reader will recognize someone he or she knows in the experiences these brave young people relate here. Those closest to the substance abuser usually get the first clues that something is wrong, but that friend or family member may experience only hurt or disappointment, not recognizing that the real problem is substance abuse. This book may help someone close to a substance user to feel less responsible, less crazy, or less hopeless. It's important to learn that no one can help a young person with a substance-abuse problem until the user admits that he or she has a problem and then asks for help. Before that point, most things done to "help" usually have the opposite effect. Once the drug user no longer denies the problem, he or she is ready for support from professionals, family, and friends. It will be needed.

If you identify with these stories or believe that you may be heading toward addiction, this book will serve as a guide to entering recovery, the process that reverses dependence upon an addictive substance. Just knowing that it is possible to combat an addictive illness, or having the example of someone else who has successfully entered recovery, makes it easier to begin the process yourself.

The Sources for Help and Information section at the back of this book will be useful for anyone who wants more information or is looking for where to go for help. It is never too soon to get off the road to addiction. And it is never too late.

Those people who showed up in my local hospital attempting to change their lives and end their years of suffering became the inspiration for this book. It is written for all of them, and also for the many young people who seem eager to take their place, who are still out there saying, "No way I'm an addict!"

IT CAN'T HAPPEN
TO ME

I was never satisfied with anything. Life in this little town was really the pits growing up, so when kids I knew started partying, I jumped right in. I might have been nine or ten when I started hanging out with older kids. Mostly we just drank. It wasn't until I was about eleven that I started smoking marijuana. I was already smoking cigarettes by then, so I'd just stash joints in the pack, and the cigs explained the burn marks on my fingers. Except for a couple of kids using LSD, we pretty much stuck to pot and alcohol.

I didn't begin to use cocaine until high school. That's when things really began to escalate. At first, we were just snorting coke, a line or two at a time. The older kids diluted it so much before they sold it

(15)

to us that it wasn't very good. But right about that time crack started to show up at my school. That was a whole different story.

Crack cocaine is very potent stuff. The first time I smoked I wanted to keep going and never stop. I felt like I would do anything just to keep the pipe lit. Every other part of my life shut down, like a deflated balloon. It was like there was no air anywhere except what I could draw through the pipe. It was overpowering the very first time.

—Danny

Every day millions of young people are exposed to drugs. They are advertised and depicted in various media, available on countless street corners, in schools and gyms, sitting in medicine, liquor, and kitchen cabinets in the home. Every young person has to make a decision each time he or she is exposed to an addictive substance. And because of the potential for harm these substances hold, it is important that every young person make the right choice about whether or not to take a drink or a drug.

Every choice a person makes has consequences. These consequences, both good and bad, help young people learn to set safe limits and make better choices. People can grow from both their successes and failures as long as they are willing to take responsibility for the consequences of their actions. Let's say, for example, that a person makes a choice to drive above the speed limit. That choice leads to the consequence of getting a speeding ticket. The driver then has to take responsibility for the choice to speed by paying the fine, and that helps him or her to learn to slow down. Even though getting pulled over and being fined are negative consequences, they actually help make the road safer, both for the driver and others who use the road.

This learning process doesn't work as well when a young person makes the choice to use alcohol or other drugs. Because these substances *intoxicate*, or poison, the brain, they interfere with thinking and feeling. This makes a user less aware of the consequences of his or her decision to pick up that drink or drug. Instead of learning to create safer limits, he or she loses safety and makes more bad decisions—and they only keep getting worse. The brain is never as clear as before the first drink or drug.

Young people have a need to assert their individuality, to find ways to be unique in a world that threatens to flatten their spirits. Harrison, for one, felt that pressure to stand out from the crowd.

> *I felt a lot of pressure to be different, to make sure I wasn't going to be just like everybody else or, worse yet, end up like my parents. The kids who used LSD in our school dressed different, acted different. I wanted to be part of that world, to make sure I stood out from everybody else.*
>
> —*Harrison*

(17)

Young people try on all sorts of behaviors, many copied from adults, trying to develop a unique personality. The drugs that Harrison and others choose to use—a certain brand of cigarette, a type of alcoholic beverage, a specific drug—all become badges to express their difference from others who don't use the same substance.

What actually happens to young people who choose to use substances is quite different. Because of the addictive nature of these drugs, users are no longer free to make choices independent of that substance. Once "hooked," they have to keep using. They become like everybody else whose life is centered around that addictive drug or behavior. This lack of independent choice also interferes with a young person's ability to move successfully into the adult world.

Brandon was strongly influenced by peers to begin drinking.

It was always very important to me to be accepted by my friends. This is a small town, so when you don't fit in with the crowd, there is nowhere else to go. In junior high, when other kids I was hanging with started to drink and smoke pot, I did too. If I didn't join in, I wouldn't have any friends. The fads changed, like it was straight shots of schnapps for a while, then Guinness stout. I partied with my friends every weekend.

Not long after I started, I was hitting the
liquor cabinet at my dad's house. He had
all kinds of booze from entertaining his
yacht club friends. I started drinking alone,
then even getting high on pot alone. By
the time I was fifteen, I was getting high
just about every day.

—*Brandon*

Brandon's story is not unique. Too often, teenagers—and adults, too—feel so much pressure to conform to those around them that they begin using drugs even if they know it's not a great idea. Because all of their friends are in the same situation, they fail to see the warning signs that things—at school, with their families, in relationships—are beginning to go wrong.

Without experiencing addiction yourself, you may find it almost impossible to understand the power that addiction has over a person's thinking, personality, and life. Nothing can really prepare someone for the changes this disease creates in one's attitudes, self-image, and intimate relationships. And because addiction usually takes hold very gradually, its effects can go unnoticed until some radical outside event jolts the situation into a user's awareness.

This was the case for Brandon and Nicole, who only became aware of their problem when faced with the consequences of their addictive behaviors. Brandon didn't wake up to the fact that he had a substance-abuse problem until the police arrested him for bur-

(19)

glary after he tried to steal liquor from a neighbor's summer home.

Nicole, a young woman who got pregnant early in her junior year of high school, has a similar story. She, too, was unaware of the consequences of her drug use until she lost custody of her child.

I was already pretty heavily into partying by the time I got to be a senior. Even though I had no trouble getting into bars, I was never very interested in drinking. It was the general rowdiness of the bars I loved. That and the fact that there were lots of older guys there, and lots of cocaine.

I would start by letting some guy buy me a few drinks, and wait until he got interested in me. Then I would tell him that I was into coke, and if he could score some, I'd be interested in splitting it with him. Usually, if the guy was pretty tanked by then, he would go for it. And cocaine is pretty easy to get in most bars; there's always someone snorting or firing up in the bathroom at most places I've been. So when the guy would score some coke, we would leave.

Once I came down from a three-day run and had no idea where I was. I had gone out Friday night and forgot all about going home. All I knew was that I was totally trashed. When I got home, I realized that I'd left my daughter with a babysitter the first night. By then someone had called child welfare on me for neglecting my child. The cops were waiting for me when I got home. I ended up losing my daughter and going to jail on the same day.

—*Nicole*

None of these young people believed that their drinking or drug taking was a problem. But each had developed—slowly but surely—a dependence on the powerful effect they received from drinking or doing drugs. This is what we call *addiction*. Addiction is a relationship with any mood-altering substance or behavior that has potentially life-threatening consequences. The most common addictions are to mood-altering chemicals like nicotine, alcohol, marijuana, heroin, or cocaine. People can also become addicted to the highs they get from certain behaviors, such as gambling, risk taking, and using highly stimulating media such as pornographic videos or violent video games.

Although the process by which people become addicted is essentially the same, this book will focus on chemical dependence, the addiction to substances taken into the body. Individual substances and the consequences of their use are explained in the two chapters on drugs of choice (chapters three and four).

Addiction doesn't come with either a warning label telling us the danger signs to watch for or with instructions on what to do when things go wrong. But it does come with a built-in mechanism that makes it easy to resist becoming aware of the problems caused by chemical dependence. This process of resisting the awareness of the consequences of drug and alcohol use is called *denial*.

Denial allows a drug user to continue using even as more time and energy are spent to obtain and use the drug. It acts like a set of blinders that prevents the user from seeing the damage caused by his or her addictive behavior. Even if some of those consequences eventually catch up—being grounded, school suspensions, arrests—denial helps the drug user blame parents or the teacher or the police for the negative consequences.

Young people exposed to substance abuse by a parent or an older brother or sister, even if they are aware of the pain that person's behavior has caused them, are actually at greater risk for becoming addicted themselves. Young people who grow up around addiction learn to survive in an environment where the use or abuse of alcohol or drugs is normal. So ignoring their own chemical dependence becomes second nature—they've already learned to ignore someone else's. The next chapter explores in greater detail just how family history affects the risk of addiction.

Dawn denied her own problem of chemical dependence for a long time, thanks in part to her own family's history. Her mother abused Xanax, a prescription medication for panic attacks, which also made it difficult for her mother to set limits on Dawn's out-of-control behavior without the intervention of the juvenile probation department.

Around my sophomore year I was smoking crack maybe every day, and I wasn't showing up for school anymore. The school filed a CHINS (Child in Need of Services) petition on me and I had to go see a probation officer. I went every week to see her, and this woman kept asking me if I was doing drugs. She said she didn't want to bust me, she was just convinced that I was screwing up my life and she wanted me to get into treatment. And every week I kept telling her, "No way I'm getting high," when that's all I was doing.

I'm not surprised that she didn't believe me. What shocked me was when I realized that I believed me! I had convinced myself that getting high every day and the lowlifes I was hanging around with had nothing to do with me not showing up for school or any of the trouble I was in.

I know now that my probation officer knew much more about what was going on than I did. It was all around me and I just couldn't see it.

—Dawn

Dawn's situation illustrates the special relationship between substance abuse and denial. The young people who have the most urgent need to recognize the problem have the most difficult time seeing it. Even those who have grown up around substance abuse, like Dawn, find it difficult to recognize the warning signs in their own lives, even when confronted with them directly.

The toll addiction takes on a young person's life and relationships is similar no matter what the drug of choice. Although there are individual differences in the effects of different drugs and the symptoms of their prolonged use, you may have noticed certain similarities in the stories of the young people you've just read. This list of features common to most forms of substance abuse should help you become more familiar with some of the physical and emotional aspects of addiction.

• *Preoccupation with substances* A lifestyle that revolves around drugs or alcohol, including posters or music about drugs or alcohol, the equipment needed to administer the drug (called drug paraphernalia), and a social life that involves their use almost exclusively.

• *Protecting the supply* The constant activity necessary to ensure access to drugs or alcohol, which includes stashing drinks or drugs around the house, taking them to work or school, frequently obtaining more, or substituting alcohol or another substance if the drug of choice is not available.

• *Increased tolerance* Using more and more of a substance to obtain or maintain the same effect, sometimes referred to as "chasing the high."

• *Power hitting* Ingesting large quantities of a drug or alcohol at one time, such as chugging an entire bottle, binge drinking five or more drinks at a sitting, or smoking a number of rocks of cocaine in succession.

• *Using alone* Using drugs or alcohol outside of a social situation, simply to get intoxicated.

• *Using alcohol or drugs as "medicine"* When a user tells himself or herself or others that he or she "needs" this drink or drug to help overcome some problem or complaint, to relax, or to become more productive.

• *Using without planning to* Reversing a decision as to when or how much of a substance a person intends to use, such as planning not to use until the weekend and then picking up the substance on a weeknight.

• *Blackouts* Use of a drug or alcohol to the point where there is no memory of what happened afterward, possibly even no memory of using at all.

WHO BECOMES AN ADDICT?

Part of my probation is going to Alcoholics Anonymous meetings three times a week. I hear a lot of the older men talk about their drinking and they remind me of my father. I wonder now if his weekends spent drinking with his friends was a sign that he was an alcoholic. I mean, he never lost his job, he always had it together by Monday. And all his friends—doctors, lawyers, whatever—were drinking right along with him. It never occurred to me that he could be an alcoholic. I'm sure it never occurred to him.

I've often wondered if maybe this disease is genetic, whether my alcoholism was passed down like hair color or the shape of my nose. I do know that my father was very demanding, especially

*when he drank. He used to criticize
everything I did. He made me feel like I
was never good enough. Now that I'm in
AA, the older men sometimes admit that
they were that way, too, very hard on their
kids, especially their sons. I'm sure that
there's some connection.*

—Brandon

No one can predict who will become addicted and who will not. Not everyone who has a drink or experiments with a drug will automatically fall into a troubled relationship with that substance. Actually, there are more young people who abstain from mood-altering substances than who don't. Of those young people who experiment with a drug or with drinking, only a small percentage become regular users or abusers of drugs or alcohol.

It's easier to predict who *won't* have a lifelong problem with addiction. These young people have a stable home life, which includes someone setting clear limits on their behavior. They have good information about substances, both legal and illegal, and know the risks involved. Their lives are filled with activities, friends, and challenges. They are able to express a wide range of emotions and have a positive relationship with at least one adult, although it's not always a parent. All of these influences serve to make young people feel valued and worthwhile.

But for those young people who are at risk for becoming addicted, there are also some striking similarities—in their family backgrounds, in the way they handle their feelings, and in the way they feel about themselves. Certain factors in each of these areas can greatly increase the likelihood that a young person will become addicted once he or she starts using drugs or alcohol.

The "Chip Off the Old Block"

The strongest influences on our development when we're growing up are the models, roles, and messages in our families. How we deal with problems and stress, the way we feel about ourselves, what we do for entertainment—all of these are learned growing up around other members of our family. It's not until adolescence that influences outside the family start becoming more important. By then, many of our responses to the outside world have settled into comfortable patterns that are resistant to change. During adolescence we develop habits for dealing with social situations based largely on our adult models.

Raymond grew up surrounded by addiction. His father and two of his uncles were alcoholics who also got high by sniffing the fumes from paint or other toxic chemicals, called *inhalants*. His mother's younger sister had attempted many times to overcome her dependence on heroin. He recalls some of his memories of growing up in this sometimes chaotic household.

> *There were many nights my brothers and I would be trying to sleep in the back of our trailer, and I could hear my father and*

uncles drinking in the front room. Some-
times we would notice that they were also
sniffing paint. We could smell it even with
the door closed. They would get louder
and louder, and usually someone would
start a fight, and things would get pretty
crazy from there. Sometimes the sheriff
would show up to try to quiet things
down, but we never got too much sleep.

Later, when they would pass out, my
big brother and I would get up and sneak
out into the living room. We could see
where they had left the rag they had used
to sniff the paint. Sometimes their nos-
trils would be silver or some wild color
from the paint. My brother and I would
finish off their half empty beers and run
back to bed.

—Raymond

Parents and older siblings are role models, and their
presence is very important to a young person's development. If a parent or other significant family member uses substances, their absence—either physically,
emotionally, or through intoxication—affects all close
relationships in destructive ways. This is what we
mean when we say that addiction is a family disease:
One person's addictive behavior affects everyone else
in that family. In such families, children cope with the
turmoil and the lack of positive attention by holding
themselves responsible. They blame themselves for

(29)

not getting what they need or for the lack of attention and approval.

A parent or an older brother or sister who makes a drink or a drug more important than their child or sibling causes that child to believe that he or she is "worth less" than the drink or the drug. A parent's substance abuse may make it impossible to set consistent limits on the child's behavior and increases the risk of that child being physically and emotionally abused. Eventually that child begins to believe that he or she is not worth being loved and cared for.

These mistaken beliefs about self-worth inherited from childhood limit the range of emotions or behaviors a young person can comfortably express. Lack of self-worth interferes with growth and learning, and personality can narrow into a distinct role, or *stereotype*. Stereotypes are like a script that cuts young people off from what they are really feeling. They are forced to leave out what doesn't fit the part they've chosen or been assigned within the family. Each of the following stereotypes places a young person at risk for beginning to have problems with substance abuse.

The "Rescuer"

Some young people attempt to distract themselves from the substance abuse in their family by being the center of attention. They may have spectacular achievements, such as making straight A's or playing competitive sports. These "overachievers" are driven, highly competitive young people who never seem to have time for themselves. They believe that they can solve any problem by trying harder. Their fantasy is that they can mend all the pain and hurt around them by being perfect.

Michelle, who later became addicted to speed, talks about her relationship with her parents and her attempt to rescue the whole family from her mother's alcohol dependence.

> *I wanted so much to make my parents happy, especially my mother. When she drank, she just hid in her bedroom, which was like her private sanctuary. There were whole days she stayed in there, just drinking and watching TV. So I took over making meals and cleaning up, and hung out a lot with my father. I tried to make up for her not being there.*
>
> *I was into gymnastics then, but I couldn't get her to come to any meets. It was always just me and my father. When he would take me out to eat somewhere after a competition, it felt funny that it was just the two of us. Sometimes it felt like my mother wasn't part of our family at all.*
>
> *—Michelle*

Michelle is like many other young people at risk for abusing laxatives or diet pills in their quest for the perfect body. Many young athletes are pressured to build their bodies to increase performance, and they may be at risk to abuse steroids. Overachievers may use amphetamines (speed) to sustain their breakneck pace or spend what free time their commitments allow partying as hard as they do everything else, maxing out on cocaine, designer drugs, or alcohol. Trying to be perfect is frustrating, which often leads to the use of substances as an escape from the pressure.

The "Scapegoat"

Often, young people respond to chaotic family situations by blaming themselves for the things that are missing. The young person who takes the scapegoat role believes that "it's my fault because I am no good." He or she sets out to provide a justification for the family's problems by getting in trouble. These are the "underachievers" who fail in school despite their high potential, or who, without planning to, get themselves or their partner pregnant.

After Danny dropped out of high school, he attended an alternative high school for a few months at the urging of his parents and to be with his girlfriend, Dawn. He was suspended when he was discovered dealing drugs in the school as a way to support his crack addiction.

I admit it was stupid, but I was stuck, you know? I had this huge habit, I was strung out on crack, and this dealer tells me that I can get my rock for free if I just move a little product for him around the school. He knows that everyone I hang with gets high. It seemed like a good idea at the time, but my thinking was pretty wacked

out when I was using. It wasn't such a
good idea when I got thrown out of the
alternative school. It was my only con-
nection to the real world. After that, things
fell totally apart.

—Danny

Young people like Danny are attracted to using drugs
both as a way of getting relief from their many failures
and as a lifestyle. They don't hide their use—they ad-
vertise it on T-shirts and by hanging out with a crowd
that is easily identified as drug users. For a scapegoat,
getting busted for drugs reinforces his or her role as a
bad person in the eyes of the family and peers, and it
confirms the belief that everything is his or her fault.

The "Entertainer"

Another role taken by young people who are at risk
for substance abuse is that of the entertainer. They
attempt to get relief and distraction from their problems by being the center of attention. These are the
class clowns, the people who are always "on stage."
They seem to be able to focus attention on themselves
no matter what is falling down around them.

Colette, who had always been shy, remembers
the powerful lure of being the center of attention when
she first started drinking.

So when I was sixteen, sometime in that
winter, was the first time I had a drink. It
was in my house. Everyone else was
fine—they were taking it slow. I remem-

(33)

ber we had sixteen-ounce beers, and I had five of them. I was not feeling good about myself, so I got completely drunk. Everyone thought I was so funny, but I was really making a big fool of myself.

Everything I said was so funny, they thought I was hilarious. So that approval, that feedback—I'd never felt that way before—like everyone liked me. So that just kind of started it. People wanted to be around me, it was amazing. That opened the door.

—Colette

Young people like Colette are often deeply troubled, but they are cut off from their feelings. They continue to show a happy face to everyone else and pretend that the problems they have at home or school don't exist. It's easy to see how this young person would be drawn to using substances as a way to blur the difference between the way she appears on the outside and the sadness she feels inside.

The "Lost Child"

Another common stereotype of a young person at risk for abusing substances relies on the opposite of distraction— isolation. The "lost child" believes "I am so worthless that I should just disappear." This idea might come from a physically absent, or a physically present but addicted, parent or from older siblings whose addiction prevents them from giving positive messages as to the younger child's worth.

The lost child is not easy to spot. Like in the movie *Home Alone*, these are the kids no one notices when they're missing. They tend to blend in with their surroundings, as if apologizing for taking up too much space. Their lonely world prevents them from experiencing the joys of intimacy with friends and family, and they become an easy target of peer pressure, feeling that they must fit in and follow the crowd.

Harrison, whose alcoholic father often stayed out drinking all night, had no adult in his life who could set limits on his out-of-control behavior.

> *I would stay out late, really late, getting high with people I'd meet in the city or just wandering around. My dad had moved out a few years before, and Mom was working all day, so she was passed out after the evening news. No one knew where I was, or even that I was gone. I would come in at three or four in the morning, the trick being to not be so stoned that I woke everybody up. In the morning I'd just tell everyone I got in around midnight. I don't think anyone knew. I don't think anyone even cared.*
> —Harrison

Without approval and guidance from caregivers, low self-worth can narrow the choices a child makes. As the child grows into adolescence, he or she may lack the confidence needed to take the risks necessary for developing independence or following through on goals. Instead of confidence, the lost child is filled with a sense of failure and impending doom. This young person will attempt to fill that emptiness by using the drugs others around him or her are using. In fact, hanging out with other drug users may give the lost child a sense of belonging that he or she has never known anywhere else.

The "Tough Guy" or "Tough Girl"

Another strong predictor of problems with addictive substances is the inability to accept help. When a young person has been let down repeatedly by parents or older family members, it is hard for him or her to trust anyone. Rather than risk disappointment again, the young person pretends that he or she can handle any problems that arise.

Prior to his arrest, Brandon had a hard time believing that he had a problem with alcohol.

> *Before I got busted in my neighbor's house, I'd been picked up by the local cops lots of times. They used to put us in protective custody. It was supposed to be such a big deal, but we all laughed about it. They would bust up a party where we had been drinking or smoking pot, and would drive us around to try and scare us and then take us to our parents. One cop tried to tell me what happens when you get strung out on drugs, about picking drunks up off the sidewalk. I remem-*

ber thinking "No way, that's not gonna happen to me." If we were older they could have locked us up, but because we were underage it was all a big joke.

—*Brandon*

Young people who share Brandon's "I can handle it" attitude believe that they can control their drinking or drugging. For them, addictive substances appear to hold a solution to all their problems: loneliness, insecurity, boredom, stress. But the more they become dependent on substances, the more isolated they become from healthy kinds of support.

Dawn spent a lot of time in high school hiding behind her "tough girl" role.

I realize now that I had lots of people who could have set me straight, but I just wouldn't listen. I knew more than anybody else. Plus I was too busy digging the hole I was in deeper and deeper.
My mother was so out of it the whole time I was growing up, I really believed that if I could survive that, I didn't need anything from anybody. When something hurt, I'd just clam up. I wouldn't even tell Danny, and he was my boyfriend.

—*Dawn*

The inability to ask for help moves the "tough guy" or "tough girl" along the road to addiction. These sub-

(37)

stance users will refuse treatment, even if they know they have a problem, because they believe that they can handle it or that no one cares or that people can't be counted on to help even if they do care. And without outside support, recovery from addiction is impossible.

Some features of all these roles may be present in the lives of young people who are using drugs or alcohol. Often, two or more stereotypes may alternate back and forth. But each of these roles is limiting and rigid, and increases the risk that a young person may embark on the path to chemical dependence.

DRUGS OF CHOICE
PART I

All addictive substances are similar in many ways. They all cause a change in body chemistry, which affects the brain either quickly or slowly, depending on the chemical makeup of the substance and the way it is taken into the body. Because addictive substances work consistently, a person comes to expect that change when he or she uses the drug. When the amount is too great or substances are used in combination, there is a very real risk of overdosing on the drug or drugs. Symptoms vary with the substance or combination of substances, but all overdoses are potentially lethal.

Longtime drug users become quite adept at computing dosages and combinations of drugs to get different effects from these substances. That's why accidental overdose happens more often to beginners—they don't know how much is too much. But any pharmaceutical in sufficient quantity can kill, even alcohol. Most young people die from an overdose of legal drugs, either from binge drinking or from sampling the medicine cabinet.

Drug distribution (except for alcohol, nicotine, and prescription and over-the-counter medications) is illegal, so there is little quality control and no guarantee of safety. Sometimes, changes in the strength, or *potency*, of a substance will cause overdoses even in longtime users. Recently, an influx of especially strong brown heroin from Mexico caused the deaths of many addicts on the East Coast. Most were long-term daily users who, after injecting the amount of their usual dose, stopped breathing. The unexpected potency of the drug caused an overdose, and they died if they had not been given immediate medical attention.

Different methods of ingestion—swallowing, inhaling, smoking, injecting into a muscle or a vein—affect the rate at which the substance starts working to alter body chemistry. That difference between when the drug is taken and when the user perceives its effect is its *timing*. The timing of a drug varies according to the method of ingestion, the amount taken, the drug's potency, the user's weight, and whether other substances or foods are present in the body. The timing of a drug affects how easily a young person can develop dependence on that substance, and how difficult it will be to stop using that particular substance. This is why smoking crack cocaine into the lungs—which affects the brain only a few seconds after the drug is inhaled—has a very different effect than snorting powdered cocaine into the nose, which takes

Accidental Overdose

All abused drugs can cause addiction, illness, or death, but the most lethal substances for teens are either alcohol or prescription medication taken in a binge—which is defined as five or more drinks or pills at a time. An incident in Woburn, Massachusetts, is a good example of how even first-time use can have tragic consequences.

The *Boston Globe* of March 2, 1997, reported that fourteen teenagers were "lucky to be alive" after ingesting "handfuls" of prescription pills at a Boys and Girls Club dance two nights before. They had ingested "literally hundreds of pills" of a prescription muscle relaxant, washing them down with water, soft drinks, and beer.

At a news conference at Children's Hospital in Boston, Dr. Michael W. Shannon said the massive overdose was caused by the combination of "what seemed to be an unlimited supply of pills" and children impatient to feel the euphoric effects of the drug, which can take from thirty minutes to two hours to occur. He said the number of pills taken by the teenagers ranged from two to thirty pills each. Twelve of the teens were hospitalized, all but one in critical condition.

The scene at the club was described as chaotic and horrifying by those who were there. The Boys and Girls Club dance, which was intended to keep teenagers out of trouble, became a frantic scene of emergency rescue workers treating dance goers who were "dropping like flies," as one police officer put it. A ninth-grade student at Woburn High said, "I saw people walking around all dizzy and tired. I was next to the kid who was sitting on the couch. He was unconscious and foaming at the mouth. He did fifty or so pills."

All of the victims were expected to recover from the overdose with no permanent damage. But, Dr. Shannon said, "I think all of them are very lucky to be alive."

(41)

longer to work its way through mucous membranes into the bloodstream. Nicotine, like crack cocaine, is very efficient in producing drug dependence because the effect of the chemical registers in the brain almost immediately.

Although all the drugs discussed in this chapter are harmful and addictive, their sale and use are not illegal. The two drugs that affect the lives of most teenagers, nicotine and alcohol, are sold and advertised openly. Others are medicines that are prescribed by doctors and that are obtained illegally or are sold over the counter in drugstores and are abused. These include prescription drugs such as the depressants Seconal and Valium and the stimulant Ritalin, as well as steroids and diet pills, and over-the-counter laxatives, inhalants, and many other drugs. The inhalants are primarily household products that are inhaled into the body, something their manufacturers never intended. Illegal drugs will be discussed in chapter four.

Nicotine

For most teens, the first drug encountered is nicotine. This was the case for Jenny, who started smoking cigarettes at twelve.

> *That's how it was the first time I actually inhaled. And it was neat 'cause you got a buzz from it. We had never drunk then, we were in the eighth grade and smoking was just something to do. And after a while we'd go out and buy one pack and split it between three of us. And finally,*

you liked it. So you just kept doing it. And then you have to do it.

—Jenny

Some people still debate whether cigarettes are addictive. Cigarettes are nicotine delivery devices: Their only purpose is to deliver a dose of a highly addictive substance so that young people will develop a chemical dependence on the drug and be hooked for life. And it's working. A 1996 survey by the University of Michigan reports that 21 percent of eighth graders, 30 percent of tenth graders, and 34 percent of twelfth graders had smoked in the previous month, which is a 10 percent increase over the previous year.

Nicotine is the drug that most affects teens: Ninety percent of the people who smoke cigarettes or use other tobacco products began using before the age of twenty. The most popular method of ingestion for teens is inhaling lit cigarettes into the lungs, followed by chewing tobacco and snuff, products made of chopped or ground tobacco that are mixed with saliva and are absorbed through the tissues of the mouth.

About one quarter of the nicotine in each puff of a cigarette reaches the brain in seven seconds. Absorption of nicotine from a dose of smokeless tobacco reaches its peak in about five minutes. Tobacco users perceive a calming effect, although actual body changes, such as increased respiration and blood pressure, mimic the effects of stress. Nicotine levels drop off rapidly, and nicotine addicts use more throughout the day to regulate their intake and to keep blood levels of nicotine constant.

Without these regular "nic-fixes," tobacco users experience symptoms of withdrawal. These can include anxiety, irritability, difficulty in concentrating, constipation, upset stomach, headaches, decreased heart rate, and drowsiness.

Short-term effects of nicotine use include bad breath, coughing, low stamina, impaired breathing, and frequent respiratory illness. Long-term effects include emphysema, chronic bronchitis, and an increased risk of heart disease, stroke, and cancers of the lung, mouth, and larynx.

Smoking, which results in 430,000 deaths every year, according to the American Lung Association, is the greatest preventable health risk nationally. But from an addiction standpoint, nicotine addiction is the most harmful because it increases the risk of addiction to other substances.

Often, young people travel along a line from the use of "legal," or *gateway drugs*, to the use of illegal substances. Gateway drugs are the substances more often used by those first experimenting with substances: tobacco, alcohol, and marijuana. Their continued abuse strongly predicts whether a user will "graduate" to other illegal substances. The director of the Center on Addiction and Substance Abuse at Columbia University, Joseph A. Calitano, Jr., was quoted in the *New York Times* on March 11, 1995, as saying that "among youths twelve to seventeen years of age, smokers were more than fifty times as likely as nonsmokers to use cocaine, and twelve times more likely to use heroin. Among adolescents who smoke heavily, the connection between cigarette smoking and other substance abuse is even stronger."

Alcohol and Other Depressants
Before she started drinking, Colette resolved that she would never drink till she was at least twenty-one. But when encouraged by friends at a party just after she turned sixteen, she gave in. Soon she was partying every weekend, and drinking more heavily than her friends were.

> *I couldn't understand why everyone else was still on their first beer, why they weren't chugging them back as quickly as possible like I was. We would each have bought a six-pack, and I would have finished my third when they were still on their first one.*
>
> —*Colette*

Alcohol is still the drug of choice among most young people, and the age at which they begin drinking is going down. According to the National Council on Alcoholism, 20 percent of the 25 million Americans who have problems with alcohol are under eighteen. A University of Michigan survey reported in 1994 that 47 percent of eighth graders, 64 percent of tenth graders, and 73 percent of twelfth graders had had at least one drink in the past year.

Depressants are substances that sedate, or put to sleep, the central nervous system. These drugs in-

(45)

clude alcohol, antianxiety and sleep medications such as Valium and Rohypnol, barbiturates like Seconal, and many of the inhalants, such as glue or paint thinner. When first ingested, they work their way into the bloodstream and then the brain, producing giddiness and euphoria while reducing anxiety. As more of the drug reaches the nervous system, the user's judgment, speech, and muscle control all become impaired.

Among teens, the most commonly abused sedative is alcohol. Despite its being legally available to persons over twenty-one, alcohol produces the same deadly combination of impaired judgment and poor muscle control common to all sedatives. The June 1994 *Journal of the American Medical Association* reports that alcohol abuse is usually involved in the deaths of adolescents by motor vehicle accidents, homicides, and suicides, and that increased drug abuse of all substances was associated with more suicidal thoughts, more serious intention to commit suicide, and more successful suicide attempts. Impaired judgment through alcohol and other drug abuse also contributes to unwanted pregnancies and sexually transmitted diseases among teens, including the increase in cases of HIV among adolescents.

Because the liver removes these toxic substances from the bloodstream much more slowly than they can be ingested, the faster these drugs and alcohol are consumed, the more likely one is to overdose. This is why "binge drinking" is so dangerous. A binge is an intentional, rapid intoxication, usually at a party, of five or more drinks in a single sitting. A Harvard University study of 17,000 college students reported that 44 percent of students had binged. The Illinois Drug Education Alliance survey in 1993 found that among high school students, 13 percent of eighth-graders had binged on at least one occasion. And parents may not be setting limits on binge drinking, at least partially due to their relief that their children are not involved with drugs that are illegal for all ages.

As the amount of alcohol or other depressant increases in the brain, the user may experience *blackouts*, or periods in which the body is active but brain functions, like reasoning and memory, are shut down. In larger doses, depressants will produce sleep, remove the sensation of pain, and, if allowed to reach high enough concentrations in the brain, shut down the involuntary muscles that control breathing and heart rate.

Recently, law enforcement officials in many states have reported an increase among teens in the use of Rohypnol, nicknamed "roofies," a sedative available in sixty countries where it is used to treat insomnia. Although not legal in the United States, it is being smuggled into the country, and has been implicated in sexual assaults in which an unsuspecting victim was rendered unconscious by a tablet planted in a drink. The combination of alcohol and Rohypnol can cause blackouts, and victims often have trouble remembering that an assault even took place. In an attempt to place Rohypnol under the same controls as heroin, LSD, and other dangerous drugs, Bob

Butterworth, the Florida attorney general, stated in June 1996 that "roofies have become the stealth weapon of choice for many sexual predators. Add to that the threat of abuse by schoolchildren and people driving under the drug's devastating influence and you have a recipe for widespread disaster."

The usual course of alcohol or depressant dependence differs for each person. Some may use these substances socially or by prescription without ever abusing them. Others may become addicted in adolescence, and begin a cycle of gradual dependence, physical and emotional deterioration, stopping use and periods of sobriety, then relapse into using again. This pattern may last their entire lifetime.

For persons who use alcohol or depressants daily, even for a few months, stopping their use suddenly is very dangerous. Withdrawal from depressants can trigger delirium tremens, a condition marked by disorganized behavior, hallucinations, violent shaking, and the possibility of seizures. Long-term use of alcohol affects every system in the body, putting the user at risk for liver and kidney disorders, esophageal lesions, inflammation of the pancreas, malnutrition, and disorders of the nervous system, including dementia, a permanent form of brain damage.

Steroids
Athletes are at risk for the abuse of drugs for many reasons. They are under tremendous pressure from parents, coaches, and teammates to succeed—at whatever cost. Their dedication to long hours of practice isolates them from typical outlets for stress, and it

can interfere with a normal social life. Drugs for many young athletes are a shortcut to relaxation and a way to cope with the stress of competition. But their greatest risk is in the abuse and possible addiction to substances used to enhance performance: pain medications, stimulants, and anabolic steroids.

When Brandon joined his varsity wrestling squad, he was very strong, but he was prevented from becoming a serious competitor because of his small size. He began using steroids under the influence of older members of the team, who also provided him with a supply.

People think that sports is gonna stop kids from doing drugs. My coach knew that most of us on the wrestling team were using steroids. He never brought it up, but there was pressure on us to build up muscle, to put on weight as fast as possible, and the older guys made sure we knew how. There is a whole network in sports for pills—steroids, speed. We could get anything. Some kids didn't want to, but there is just too much pressure to win. And all the adults—coaches, referees, even parents—made sure to look the other way.

—Brandon

Many college and even high school athletes report that drugs are available, and that their use is often encouraged, to increase muscle size, to permit them to play when tired or injured, and to heighten performance. Because coaches and older players are powerful role models, this pressure to use substances to win at all costs is difficult to resist. Young athletes know the risks of using these drugs, but believe the risks are worth it or that the side effects will happen to someone else, not to them. The muscular bodies that result from steroid abuse help to convince them that they are invincible.

Brandon very quickly learned to depend upon steroids, not only for the changes they helped him accomplish physically, but for the way those changes made him feel.

> *What really surprised me was not that it worked, but how great it made me feel to be really pumped up. I got so much more attention from the guys on the team, more respect. And the girls—I became like a babe magnet. I wasn't ready for how big a difference using steroids made, it really went to my head.*
> *—Brandon*

Our current obsession with the body is fueled by pictures of athletic physiques in fashion layouts and advertisements in the mainstream media. Both men and women are depicted as sex objects, and many young people will try anything that promises to deliver a body that will gain them approval and attention.

Anabolic steroids are related to the male sex hormone, testosterone, and are usually prescribed af-

(50)

ter a serious illness or an injury to help rebuild muscle mass. For an otherwise healthy young person, steroids produce quick gains in weight and muscle mass, in contrast to much slower development through exercise and nutrition alone. Typically, abuse starts with either pills or injections into the muscles of the buttocks. Side effects, which can include outbreaks of acne on the upper back, rashes, baldness, shrunken testicles, reduced sexual drive, heavier beards, and puffy faces, develop gradually. The onset of these side effects prompts many to stop using steroids.

Once off the drug, users rapidly lose the weight they had gained, and many become depressed over the loss of size, athletic ability, and the attention that went with their steroid-enhanced body. Often, they will start another cycle, continuing the pattern of use, weight gain, side effects, cessation, weight loss, and emotional withdrawal. This pattern is similar to cycles experienced by persons with eating disorders whose weights fluctuate wildly up and down.

Anabolic steroids have been linked to increases in aggressive behavior in habitual users. These sudden emotional outbursts, called "'roid rages," often escalate to violence with little provocation. This was the case for Brandon, who assaulted another student while under the influence of steroids and was subsequently arrested for assault and dropped from wrestling by his school.

Long-term use of steroids can cause heart disease, increased risk of liver tumors, and damage to the endocrine system. Users also run the risk of accidentally ingesting different and often harmful chemicals, because legal channels for obtaining the anabolic steroids don't exist.

Inhalants

Inhalants are substances found in household and industrial products that are inhaled, or "sniffed," for the purpose of intoxication. The hundreds of complex chemical compounds that have potential for inhalant abuse can be divided into three types: solvents including toluene, gasoline, paint thinner, and airplane glue; aerosol products including butane and other propellants used in spray paints, insecticides, and hair spray; anesthetics including nitrous oxide, or "laughing gas," and ether. These substances are put into a paper bag, or on a rag, or are sprayed into a balloon or into an empty soft drink can and the toxic fumes inhaled. The effect is similar to the depressants discussed before.

Young people often start experimenting with inhalants at a younger age than other substances, possibly due to their availability. Raymond, who was surrounded with older inhalant abusers, was one of these.

The first time I sniffed paint was one of those nights after they had all passed out. I picked up the rag lying next to my uncle, who was snoring away. I started to inhale, and my brother looked at me like I was crazy.

By the time I was twelve, I was sniffing paint and glue with my friends all the time. I got high with one of my uncles a few times, although I'm not sure he even remembers. He was pretty far gone by then. I knew that it rotted out your brain, but that didn't stop me. I figured it wouldn't happen to me.

—*Raymond*

Inhalant abuse is more prevalent among certain ethnic populations, notably Native American and Mexican American youths. Many inhalant abusers also experiment with other substances, usually alcohol and pot. The effect of multiple substance use at such a young age on mental and emotional development is still unknown.

Symptoms of inhalant abuse include coughing, memory loss, irritated nasal passages, kidney disease, perforations in the liver, heart irregularities, permanent nerve damage, cognitive impairment, and increased risk of cancer. Long-term use can result in irreversible dementia, marked by violent outbursts, impaired learning skills, and low motivation to change. Because of this, long-term inhalant abusers are not easily placed in treatment.

DRUGS OF CHOICE
PART II

This chapter focuses on illegal or illicit drugs, also called "controlled substances" because laws prohibit their possession and sale. These are processed natural products like marijuana, heroin, and cocaine or chemicals like LSD or "ecstasy" designed to induce addictive behavior and to make huge profits for those who manufacture and distribute them.

Also included in this chapter are legally produced prescription pain medications, such as Vicodin and codeine, because they are similar in chemical action and addictive potential to illegal narcotics. Despite strict controls to prevent these substances from being abused, large amounts of these substances are routinely distributed illegally.

Obtaining and using "controlled substances" is classified as a criminal act. Except for some experimental programs using marijuana to relieve symptoms of nausea associated with chemotherapy and the syndrome of acquired immune deficiency, or AIDS, there is no way to obtain these drugs without risking arrest and subsequent prosecution. Laws prohibit underage users from obtaining alcohol or tobacco products and prescription drugs, but the penalties for buying and using "legal" drugs are much less severe. Because of the tremendous profits to be made in illegal drug trafficking, whole underground networks of production and distribution of these substances have sprung up worldwide. These "drug cartels" cross national boundaries, spreading substances primarily from poorer, Third World countries to sell in the richer, industrialized countries of Europe and North America. Some of these organizations maintain private armies that ruthlessly kill those who oppose their drug enterprise: judges and journalists, police and military personnel, competing drug dealers, and their own members deemed to be disloyal. There is also evidence that money from the drug trade helps supply guns and explosives to terrorist groups.

In addition, there is a documented connection between the spread of drug trafficking to an area and the increase in gun violence. Two related stories in the *New York Times* of December 13, 1994, suggested that "guns multiplied right after the crack came," and that the use of crack was directly linked to an increase in the number of young people killed in areas where the drug became available. As well-armed gangs fight each other for turf—literally, the territory where they control illicit drug sales—many gang members, as well as their innocent neighbors and younger brothers and sisters, get killed in the crossfire. But this is only the most visible part of the destructive effect of the drug trade. There are deep wounds in the culture everywhere these substances are produced or distributed.

Attempts to limit drug distribution and sales have only been marginally successful at stopping the access young people have to addictive substances. The high school health teacher in a tiny suburban town near me reports that heroin is cheaper in his school than in the large industrial town to our north where most of the local adult addicts go to score. Billions of dollars are spent by young people each year on legal and illegal substances alike. But the real cost is measured not in dollars, but in lost opportunities, lost years, and lost lives. Only when young people themselves get angry enough about being enslaved for the gain of others will the drug problem be solved.

Marijuana and Hashish
Marijuana, the most popular illegal drug for all Americans, is showing increased use among high school students for the first time in twenty years. The Institute for Social Research at the University of Michigan in their "Monitoring the Future" survey found in 1996 that 36 percent of twelfth graders and 34 percent of tenth graders had smoked pot. Among eighth graders, the number smoking pot was 18 percent, having tripled over a five-year period.

Harrison was one of those kids who started smoking pot before he entered high school.

I was thirteen, I think, when I started smoking pot. It was a pretty hazy summer before ninth grade. I was playing guitar, hanging out with older neighborhood kids, and this one guy who played harmonica kind of took care of me. It felt good to be included, especially with the big kids. Where they went, I went. When they drank, I drank. And when somebody fired up a joint, I got right in line.

—Harrison

Typically, the dried leaves of the pot plant are smoked in hand-rolled joints, hollowed-out cigarettes called "blunts," or in a pipe, but are also ingested in food, like cookies or brownies. Hashish is a concentrated form of the plant resins, and it is also smoked or eaten. Their active ingredient, tetrahydrocannabinol or THC, is absorbed into the bloodstream. There it begins to affect the brain, primarily in the areas that affect movement and memory. THC also affects the circulatory system, dilating veins and arteries and speeding up heart rate.

Users experience a range of responses, from relaxation and sleepiness to extreme disorientation and panic. Getting "stoned" impairs judgment, short-term memory, balance, perception, and muscle coordination. Delusions and hallucinations are sometimes

(57)

present. Highs usually last only a few hours, but it takes weeks for the liver to eliminate all the THC from the body. Tars and other chemicals in the smoke affect the respiratory system more quickly than smoking tobacco, decreasing lung capacity and irritating the bronchi, throat, and lungs.

Consistent use of marijuana or hashish decreases motivation and energy level, which interferes with work, school, sports, and social interaction. Pot smokers tend to associate with other pot smokers, getting further cut off from the world outside the "drug culture." Though marijuana is not as physically addictive as other substances, its users tend to become very dependent emotionally upon the effects of the drug and often experience a great loss of potential in all areas of their lives.

Harrison was an A student at the beginning of high school, but by senior year his pot smoking put him at risk for dropping out altogether and also to start using other substances.

I went along, smoking pot for a long while, but my friend Dougie started taking all kinds of things—LSD, mostly, and cocaine—and wanted me to do some with him. I was afraid of getting hooked smoking cocaine, but nobody seemed to be addicted to LSD.

When I finally dropped acid, I said, "This is the real thing." It was like getting stoned on the best dope, but without

coughing your lungs out. Pretty soon that
became our routine: Pot every day and
acid on weekends.

—*Harrison*

According to a 1995 report based on current patterns of drug use among young people by the Center on Addiction and Substance Abuse, twelve- to seventeen-year-olds who reported using marijuana were eighty-five times more likely to later use cocaine than their age mates who never smoked pot. The younger the person when they first used marijuana, the more likely it was that they went on to use cocaine, heroin, hallucinogens, and other illicit substances. While this does not prove that using a gateway drug such as marijuana will cause dependence on other substances, it does predict that a young person is much more likely to try these illegal substances if there is prior use of tobacco, alcohol, or marijuana.

Cocaine and Other Stimulants
Like many of the illegal drugs, cocaine users often "graduate" to smoking or snorting coke after first using another substance, usually tobacco, alcohol, or marijuana. For Danny, it was all three.

Of course it was easier to start smoking
crack—I already knew how to inhale.
Plus, I had been fooling my parents by
burning incense in my room and puffing
out the window so they wouldn't know I

was smoking cigarettes, and then pot. I just did the same thing when I started smoking crack.

—Danny

Cocaine is one of a class of drugs that include amphetamines, or "speed," diet pills, methcathinone, or CAT, and caffeine. Caffeine and pill forms of amphetamines are swallowed; powdered forms of cocaine and speed can be inhaled or injected intravenously. Powdered cocaine can be heated and the vapors inhaled in a process called free basing, but this method has been replaced by crack, small rocks of cocaine, which can be smoked more easily.

Amphetamines, the most commonly abused stimulants, are distributed in a variety of pills. Small "white crosses" and Dexedrine capsules are common. Amphetamines are also found in a powdered form called "crystal meth," short for crystallized methamphetamine, which has recently appeared in a smokable form called "ice." There are also synthetic stimulants like CAT, also known as "crank," that run the added risk of unknown potency and possible contamination by other substances. Finally, there is "legal speed," which are various natural and synthetic compounds, often mostly caffeine. These over-the-counter pills are openly advertised in fitness and men's magazines and are usually packaged to look like the amphetamines legally manufactured by drug companies.

Stimulants increase the activity of neurotransmitters, chemical messengers in the brain. Small doses

(60)

increase alertness and energy, while blocking the sensations of appetite and fatigue. Most swallowed or snorted stimulants are slow to take effect, last a number of hours depending upon the dose, and are followed by feelings of despondency, depression, and low motivation.

Taken in small amounts, cocaine has an effect similar to other stimulants. But in larger doses, cocaine activates centers in the brain that register feelings of reward and well-being, causing the user to feel powerful and self-confident.

This effect lasts only a few minutes, followed by a "crash" that results in feelings of depression and intense cravings for more of the drug. This is especially true for users who smoke or inject the drug because of how quickly the drug affects brain chemistry, which is usually only a few seconds. Some crack users have reported becoming addicted after their first use.

Because of the intensely addictive nature of crack, it has created a secondary problem that also carries the risk of injury and death: crime. To support the obsession to continue using this drug, many crack addicts become involved in distributing and selling the drug. They routinely commit other types of crimes, such as burglary or prostitution.

Users of all stimulants are often irritable, anxious, and have difficulty sleeping. Long-term users can develop problems with the lining of their nasal passages or their lungs, and psychotic symptoms such as paranoia or delusions. Stimulants increase the risk of heart attack, especially in users of crack and CAT.

Withdrawal from stimulants carries the risk of seizures, and users experience strong cravings that make them want to go back on the drug. Those attempting to stop using these substances almost always require outside intervention and treatment.

LSD, PCP, and "Designer Drugs"

Like many of the fashions of the 1960s, LSD is making a comeback among high school and college students. Here, Harrison recalls what he can remember of his own experiences as a "fashion victim."

I don't really know how many hits of LSD I've taken. There were months when I dropped every weekend, and maybe a few times during the week. At first, it would take a few days for things to straighten out and I could seriously function again. Then it began to take a week before I really knew what was going on. For one short stretch I never came down. I think I graduated from high school in there somewhere, then I traveled around a bit. I seem to remember crashing in some pretty disgusting places, but it's all really hazy. I know I went to a lot of concerts, but I can't remember what the music sounded like. It's like that joke about the sixties: "If you remember the sixties, you weren't there!"

—Harrison

The collective memory of young people is not long enough to remember the havoc created by the epidemic of hallucinogens in an earlier generation. Many hundreds of young people were injured or killed as a result of using these drugs, and many thousands more "dropped out" of life, victims of the emotional and mental devastation created by these substances. Sadly, many young people like Harrison are going through this experience all over again.

A single dose of LSD taken by mouth can result in eight hours or more of altered reality, including distorted perceptions of time, space, and the user's physical limitations. Moods can change dramatically without warning, feelings are intensified, and users report confusing the senses, such as "hearing colors." Visual hallucinations are common and are sometimes terrifying.

Because of the potency and relatively low cost of LSD, users often take multiple doses, greatly compounding the risk of a "bad trip." The effect of the drug is perceived as oppressive during these periods, which are marked by free-flowing and disorganized speech, loose association of ideas, and sometimes by intense feelings of fearfulness or grief. Because these symptoms are usually indicators of serious mental illness, users of LSD and other hallucinogens have been hospitalized while high on the drug because they appeared to be psychotic.

Long-term use of LSD lowers ability on mental tasks, and often increases anxiety and paranoia. Users also report "acid flashbacks" in which hallucinations return suddenly, days or weeks after using but without having taken more of the drug.

PCP acts more quickly and for a shorter period of time than LSD, but it has a more dangerous effect. Because it is added to marijuana or tobacco and smoked, PCP enters the brain very quickly, producing a sudden rush of energy, vivid hallucinations, and a high tolerance to pain. First-time use of PCP has caused psychotic breakdowns, convulsions, heart failure, and coma. Long-term use increases the risk of mental illness, anorexia, or changes in personality that leave the user anxious, withdrawn, and prone to sudden outbursts of anger.

Because the effects of both these drugs vary from person to person, and from use to use by the same person, it is impossible to predict their influence on a user's behavior. Hallucinations that make other people seem as if they are monsters or demons have provoked violent behavior, and some users have died because they were unable to sense the danger of a passing car or of jumping from a high place.

MDMA (methylene dioxymethamphetamine), or "ecstasy," has been associated recently with dance clubs and "raves." It closely resembles a drug called MDA (methylene dioxyamphetamine) that was popular during the 1960s and 1970s. These "designer drugs" are manufactured in home labs to imitate chemically other controlled substances, in this case, both a stimulant and a hallucinogen. Their action on the body is similar to the substance they resemble, but designer drugs are of inconsistent strength and quality, and are often diluted with other substances

(64)

to stretch profits. This unpredictability of the potency, and even the identity of these substances, increases the risk of an accidental overdose. MDMA use has been linked to increased body temperature, convulsions, and death from heart failure.

Heroin and Pain Medication

Heroin is one of a class of drugs called narcotic analgesics that are used for pain relief. They work on the central nervous system to block messages that come from pain receptors. These drugs are also called "opiates," because many of them are derived from the sap of the opium poppy. They include opium, heroin, morphine, codeine, methadone, and a large number of prescription medications like Demerol, Darvon, and Dilaudid. Some, such as Vicodin and Percocet, are combinations with other medications. Like most prescription medications that are sold illegally, these are usually in pill form, but some are obtainable as liquid and can be injected intravenously. Opium is usually sold as a sticky brown gum and is usually smoked. Heroin is sold as a powder, which is either snorted into the nose or converted into liquid and injected under the skin or into a vein. Methadone is available by prescription in pill or liquid form as a way to maintain addicts on a legal supply of narcotics, but it is sometimes sold illegally and abused.

When taken, narcotics move through the body and connect with nerve endings, stimulating activity in an area of the brain known as the "pleasure center," as well as in other areas of the brain. An injection of heroin reaches these sites in about seven seconds, which is one reason people become addicted so quickly to this drug. After injecting or snorting heroin, the user is filled with an immediate rush of euphoria followed by several hours of pleasurable drowsiness. He or she often looks like someone nodding off to sleep. Other narcotic drugs act in a similar fashion, although not as quickly. While intoxicated, narcotics users are self-absorbed, mentally blunted, and sometimes cannot respond at all. When not intoxicated, they are extremely restless, unable to sleep, and are aggressively focused on obtaining more of the drug.

Almost every narcotic user reports having previously used alcohol. Most users of heroin have previously used another substance, often marijuana, but sometimes cocaine or another narcotic. Typically, a user will "graduate" to heroin from one of these substances.

Danny had abused alcohol, marijuana, the prescription sedative Xanax, and cocaine before the first time he used heroin.

> *I didn't really plan to start doing heroin. One day I couldn't score any rock, and I was starting to get sick. Someone had a bag of heroin, and I would do anything to stop feeling that bad. So I did it up, just shot it up the first time. I'd seen lots of people shoot up, and I remember saying, "I can do that." And I did.*
>
> *—Danny*

As young people like Danny move from the use of "soft" or gateway drugs to "hard" or illicit drugs, their sense of right and wrong breaks down as a result of having to cover up constantly and lie about obtaining and using illegal drugs. At first, they can justify this behavior because it keeps them from getting "busted," but, gradually, dishonesty becomes more and more routine. This breakdown in moral judgment—what a young person believes is right and wrong—can result in the user engaging in even more criminal acts to maintain a supply: dealing drugs, theft, assault, or prostitution.

Although heroin is relatively inexpensive, users will develop a daily habit running into hundreds of dollars once they become dependent upon the drug. The addict's lifestyle becomes focused entirely on meeting this demand. All other aspects of life are neglected, and many heroin addicts end up living "on the street." This marginal lifestyle may involve living in abandoned buildings or in homeless shelters, or exploiting friends and family for food and money for more drugs. Addicts often resort to petty crimes or prostitution, especially younger addicts, and many spend time in the criminal justice system. They may get free of the drug during these periods, but often pick up use of the drug again once back out on the street.

Often, heroin users will substitute a depressant or another narcotic if their drug of choice is unavailable, or they will take different substances over the course of a day or in combination—whatever is available to prevent the uncomfortable feeling of withdrawal. This increases the risk of overdose, which may include seizures, incoherent speech, agitation, restlessness, severe drowsiness, difficulty in breathing, and physical collapse.

Any drug administered by injection carries the added risk of infectious disease through shared needles. These can include serious infections like the human immunodeficiency virus (HIV), which results in AIDS, hepatitis, and tuberculosis, as well as skin infections.

THE ROAD TO ADDICTION

Looks were always very important to me. As far back as I can remember, getting approval for the way I looked made me feel really good, really special. I guess it started with my father, who was sort of a health nut—always working out and showing off how trim he was. We lived in South Florida, so I practically lived in the water. He would always compliment me on how I looked in a swimsuit, and say nasty things about other people if their bodies weren't perfect. It became a way I could get his approval, so I made sure I wasn't going to get fat.

I started using pills to diet when I was twelve, and switched over to snorting crystal meth in high school. Not only did they keep me skinny, but I liked the way

*they made me feel: like I was motivated
and in charge—capable of anything. It got
to where I needed speed to feel good.
Pretty soon I didn't do anything unless I
had snorted some crystal first. I ended up
dating an older guy who was dealing, so
it wasn't hard to get speed whenever I
wanted.*

—Michelle

Many young people who try a drug believe it can
make them feel better than they would without it.
Maybe they would like to escape temporarily from the
burden of being themselves, and believe that using
drugs and alcohol might provide that escape, or a
sense of being grown-up, or just a way to be different.
These beliefs are reinforced by the pressure of friends
who may be using drugs, and by media images of
adults drinking or using drugs to relax, fit in, or have
fun. Sometimes these young people are aware of
adults using drugs within their family.

The road to addiction moves through a number
of predictable stages, starting with developing ideas
and expectations about what a particular substance
will do. This slowly progresses to obtaining and experimenting with a substance. Then follows the stage
of regular use, in which substances become part of
the user's everyday life. Here, lifestyle and personality begin to adapt to getting, using, and hiding drugs
or alcohol.

This chapter will outline the process that leads
to addiction from a young person's first awareness of

substances right through to habitual use. The later stages of the addiction process, dependence, and life threatening use will be discussed in chapter six: Addiction.

Jenny remembers what her ideas were about smoking cigarettes before she ever smoked one, and how those ideas changed one summer vacation after seeing other kids smoke.

The one time I smoked in the fifth grade was because I wondered what it was like. Every kid is curious when they're that age. We saw our parents do it, and we wanted to try it. But it was eighth grade when we all really started.

Everyone used to smoke at this place downtown. I think the odd thing is that the two of us, me and Pam, would always go down there and break the other kids' cigarettes. We'd ask for a drag and then break their cigarettes. Finally the other kids said, "Why don't you just have one?" After a whole summer of trying to get them to quit, we just gave up. Now I've been smoking for three years and I know it's ridiculous.

—Jenny

The process of becoming addicted is different for each individual. To go from a few drags on a friend's cigarette to smoking every day may take years, or it may take only a few weeks. Some substances seem to move people much more quickly through this process than others.

This is due to the number and location of nerve endings in the brain affected by the chemical activity of the drug, and how soon after taking the drug the user feels the effect. Generally, the more parts of the brain that are affected, and the closer a drug comes to acting instantly, the more quickly a young person will move through the stages of the addiction cycle. For example, smoking crack cocaine develops dependence in its users more quickly than inhaling powdered cocaine through the nose. Either method of ingestion can get a young person addicted. All cocaine users travel down the same road, just in different lanes.

Addiction is a learning process that only moves in one direction. Just as it is impossible to "unlearn" how to swim or ride a bike, it is impossible to go from a later stage of addiction back to an earlier one. A young person who develops a habit of regular use is rarely successful in going back to infrequent use. Even occasional use will force the user to "relearn" his or her drug habit. The only way out of this process is to get some outside support to stop entirely and, if needed, get into some form of treatment.

There is often no clear line between where one stage of the addiction process ends and the next begins. The damage is not detectable until the later stages of this process, when things really start falling apart. Only then do the consequences of using drugs or alcohol become clear. By understanding the road

(72)

to addiction, and knowing where it leads, it's possible to tell sooner, rather than later, that it's time to stop.

Stage 1: Expectation and Planning
Long before he ever took a drink, Brandon had developed his own ideas about what it meant to be able to drink alcohol.

> *I think it was all about power, how the grown-ups could do whatever they wanted and told us kids what we had to do and what we couldn't. I wanted to have that power and to stop being bossed around.*
>
> *Nobody tells you when you cross that line from being a kid to being a grown-up. I figured out early on that there are two things that grown-ups can do that kids can't. One of those is driving a car, and the other is drinking. I really believed that when I got my license and was able to get liquor, I would finally be a full-fledged adult, and nobody could stop me from doing whatever I wanted. I really believed that. And when I saw kids my own age drinking, I figured that I didn't have to wait till I was twenty-one for this to happen, I'd go ahead and be a grown-up right now.*
>
> *—Brandon*

No one starts using a drug with the intention of becoming addicted. No young person wakes up one morning and says, "It's a nice day . . . I think I'll go out and smoke some crack." A relationship with a mood-altering substance begins long before that substance is used.

The problem with drugs or alcohol is not just the substance itself, but the relationship a person develops with that substance. For most young people, their relationship with drugs and alcohol starts when they first become aware that people use drugs to change their moods or behavior, and they begin to wonder what that's about. The first exposure might be a relative who is intoxicated at a family gathering, a comedian on television who pretends to be falling down drunk, or a character in fiction who uses heroin.

These pieces of information collect in that young person's mind and begin to create an idea of what it means to be intoxicated. He or she begins to wonder why someone would do that, what makes it different from how people normally behave, and how people— mainly adults—get that way. He or she may react to this exposure with fear or disgust, especially if the person using the drug is someone close, or is abusive when intoxicated. This young person may firmly believe that he or she will never get that way.

Gradually, these pieces of information form into a concept of what it means to use drugs or alcohol. It is normal, even healthy, to have information about what addictive substances do and why people use them. These substances are part of our world, and all young people need to know how to deal with them and with the people who choose to use them.

A young person may fantasize that using these substances will give him or her relief or escape, that the drugs will ease difficult social situations, or will provide him or her with entrance into an adult world of sophistication and self-assurance. Whether these things will really happen is not important. What that young person believes might happen forms the basis for his or her decisions about substances. If a young person does have an opportunity to use drugs or alcohol and makes the choice to use them, much of that experience is shaped by these expectations, especially in the beginning.

Stage 2: Experimentation
A precocious teen, Harrison fit in easily with young adults. His first experience with speed happened at an all-night party with an older crowd.

There were nights when I would go alone into Manhattan and sneak into clubs. I figured that a group of underage kids would be more suspicious, but really there was nobody I knew who was crazy enough to try it. I would try to blend in and would usually end up with a group of older people.

One night I met some people who were dancing like crazy. I figured they were pretty wired. There was always speed at

the dance clubs, sometimes the bath-
room was a regular drugstore. I ended
up going with them to a party afterward.
There was always a party afterward—
these people never slept. That's how I got
to snort speed the first time. One guy
turned me on to a couple of lines, and
we sat around and played guitar until my
fingers were bleeding.

When morning came, I took the sub-
way straight to school. I was still pretty
wired, but I started crashing about fifth
period. I went to the school nurse, but she
was particularly nasty and wouldn't let
me go home sick.

—Harrison

One of the reasons drugs hook so many people is because they work. They change body and brain chemistry soon after they are ingested, and people who use them feel different. They may not feel any better, any more adult, or any more able to deal with the difficult challenges of adolescence, but they feel something.

The experimentation stage of the addiction process is where beginning users learn how drugs work. They learn the timing of a particular drug and check out their expectations of what they thought would happen. They begin to become accustomed to the effect of the drug, and they learn to deal with the side effects: coughing, nausea, breath odor, or others, depending upon the drug. These experimenters also learn to be deceptive about their use. Lying, which before this may have been unthinkable, starts to become part of their everyday life.

One of the attractions for young people of using substances is that they serve as a form of initiation into the adult world. Beginners pick up the rituals associated with different drugs from those already using them. They clean and roll pot, chop up cocaine, become experts at pill identification, and learn to fashion pipes out of just about anything. Sadly, our culture has few rites of passage from childhood to adulthood. Leaving the teen years holds little promise for many adolescents aside from the expectation that they can get a driver's license and obtain alcohol.

Colette began drinking at about the time in her life when she was experiencing a sense of transition into adulthood.

My dad went away for a few weeks and I started having people over. I don't think anyone really pushed me to drink. It was just me and my girlfriends, my two best friends, we had no idea what it was like. One of them had tried it, and we were always competing, so I thought, "Now I have to try it."

That just kind of started it. Everything else started that year—I lost my virginity that year, I started smoking pot that year, I started smoking cigarettes that year— all when I turned sixteen.

—Colette

(77)

Most adolescents begin to experiment with various substances between the ages of twelve and fourteen, and there are a lot of them. The July 28, 1995, *CQ Researcher* reports that "close to half of America's teenagers will try an illicit drug (not including alcohol) by the time they reach twelfth grade." Only a small percentage of those young people who reach this stage of the addiction process go on to regular use or become addicted. But those who do continue down the road to addiction rarely experience difficulties at home or school at this early stage. Young people are resilient; they bounce back after a weekend binge or catch up on a lost night of sleep. It's hard for these young people or those around them to see the danger of their continued use.

The overwhelming majority of young people who try drugs or alcohol decide at this point that it's not worth it. Experimentation does not have to progress to a later stage of advanced drug abuse, and, fortunately for most young people, it doesn't. After checking out the effects of substances and finding out firsthand about the risks involved, more than 80 percent taper off and never develop an ongoing relationship with a substance. But for those who continue along the road to addiction, drugs become an everyday thing.

Stage 3: Habitual Use
Dawn, who had been somewhat of a loner, seemed to find a sense of connection when she began to use drugs regularly.

I never felt good about myself. When I started high school, I was convinced that I was the ugliest girl in class, that I'd never get a date. When I had to walk to the front of the room to hand in a paper or give a speech, I thought that everyone was looking at me. I was pretty miserable, but I hid it.

Things really changed when I started getting high. There was a crowd of people who accepted me, totally. Suddenly, I felt like I belonged somewhere. They became my family, in a way. Then I started going out with Danny, which mostly involved getting high together every day.

I didn't care anymore about what other kids thought at school or the teachers. That's when I stopped showing up for school at all. In fact, I didn't care about what anybody thought as long as I had Danny. And the drugs.

—Dawn

Adolescence is a turbulent time, filled with many changes and conflicts. When young people begin to use drugs regularly, they lose the ability to cope with these challenges in any other way. This is true for cigarettes and alcohol as well as illegal drugs because all mood-altering substances distort feelings in some way. Regular drug users have learned to use substances to feel more motivated, more alive, more special, more involved, or more connected when they use them, but it's only an illusion. That sense of control over all the random, unpredictable things that come into their lives is what drags a young person further along the road to addiction.

As teens use more frequently, especially illicit drugs, there is more deception and lying as more time and money are spent chasing the high. This breaks down trust with friends and adults, and often leads to feelings of guilt, worthlessness, and remorse. These uncomfortable feelings trigger even more drug use, creating a cycle that moves the user further down the road to addiction.

The daily use of substances affects all parts of a young person's lifestyle. Outside activities disappear as more time and energy are focused on obtaining and using substances. Participation in school, family activities, sports, or extracurricular activities begins to drop off gradually at first, then builds momentum as more parts of that young person's life drop away. There are other reasons for young people seeming to disappear from sight: They may be experiencing a serious illness, depression, an unexpected tragedy, an unhealthy dating relationship, or conflicts at home. But the isolation caused by preoccupation with drugs or alcohol is self inflicted.

At this stage, use is not casual, but follows a very predictable pattern that ensures that the drug supply is fairly constant—usually weekly or daily. Friends and activities that don't center on the addictive behavior, or those that make it difficult to continue using the substance, are cut back or "dropped out" of all together. The user focuses a great deal of time and energy on maintaining a supply of the drug of choice or substitutes another in case that one is not available. Anywhere those substances are not allowed or obtainable is avoided.

Thinking becomes distorted by regular drug use, so young people are more likely to risk unsafe sex. This can result in sexually transmitted diseases—including the very real danger of contracting HIV—and unwanted pregnancies. Teens who use drugs also make rash decisions about partners, and are more likely to be assaulted, to assault others, or to attempt suicide.

It's during this stage that drug *tolerance* develops. Tolerance is the body's tendency to become more accustomed to the effect of a particular substance—more tolerant of it—so that the drug stops working as efficiently. It takes more of the drug to produce the same effect. The user may not be aware that this change is taking place. He or she may inhale a cigarette or joint more deeply, take longer drinks from a bottle of alcohol, or run through his or her stash of pills or cocaine more quickly. The rate at which tolerance develops is different for each substance, but the result is the same. To maintain the habit, the user needs increasingly more of the drug.

Often, users will realize that things are spiraling out of control, and they may attempt to stop using the substance for a time. It is still possible at this point to taper off most drugs or alcohol without outside help.

(81)

signs

Signs That Someone You Know May Be Abusing Alcohol or Drugs

The changes that indicate someone is moving along the path to addiction are sometimes very subtle, sometimes not. Here are some common indicators of drug or alcohol abuse. If any of the following apply to you or someone you know, it may indicate a serious problem.

1. Sudden changes in mood or attitude
2. Establishing friendships with those who use drugs or alcohol regularly
3. Dropping out of extracurricular activities or giving up leisure activities
4. Not caring about grades, household jobs, or other commitments to family and friends
5. Feeling depressed much of the time
6. A change in taking care of physical needs, such as sleeping, eating, or personal hygiene
7. A sudden loss of weight
8. Difficulty being honest with others
9. Skipping school, driving recklessly, or taking household objects or money
10. Frequently losing or changing jobs
11. Spending more time alone, isolated from friends and family
12. Hiding drug paraphernalia, alcohol, or empty bottles
13. Smelling of alcohol and drugs
14. Noticeable intoxication

If you have noticed any of these signs, find out if help is needed in dealing with alcohol or drugs.

(82)

These periods of abstinence can give a false sense of security, making them feel that they are in control of their drug use. They often start up again, and their habit quickly goes back to the same or a higher level. These breaks may continue, alternating with feelings of helplessness and hopelessness when they become shorter or even nonexistent.

Someone who uses drugs regularly is not necessarily drug dependent or even guaranteed to become addicted. Daily use is an indicator of a serious drug problem, but *why* someone is using is more important than *how much* in determining if a young person will progress to the next stage of addiction and become drug dependent.

The young drug user at this stage finds himself or herself struggling with whether to move backward or forward in the addiction process. But because the road to addiction only goes one way, the habitual drug user has only two choices: to get into a substance abuse recovery program or ease on down to the next stage, drug dependence.

ADDICTION

I remember the morning I got in Dougie's old red VW and we drove out to the river on the way to school. There was traffic rushing by on one side, water on the other, and we sat there smoking pot and laughing at anything either of us said.

Coasting through school that day, nothing really mattered: grades, teachers, what the other kids thought. It was like all the pressure had lifted and was replaced by a purple haze. After that, I never made it to school without getting high. We had a joke about it. One of us would say, "Do you go to Fort Hamilton High?" and the other would say, "I couldn't make it any other way!"

—Harrison

There is a sharp division between the earlier stages of the addictive process and the last two, although the user may not perceive the change until after it takes place, if at all. The point at which habitual use becomes addiction is different for everyone, but there are some similarities. Past this point, drug or alcohol use has serious consequences, and affects all aspects of a person's life, from relationships with family and friends, to school, to self-esteem. The good feelings that used to come with using disappear, and they are replaced by negativity, depression, and helplessness. The young person's life begins to spin out of control, often to the point at which he or she is faced with social, physical, and mental breakdowns. The road to addiction has reached the two final stages of drug dependence and life-threatening use.

Stage 4: Dependence
After experimenting with using pot and other hallucinogens for some time, Harrison began cutting himself off from activities and interests he enjoyed because they interfered with getting high.

> *Somehow I made it to an All-District Chorus rehearsal that Saturday instead of hanging with my friends, because music is important to me. I remember I was having a really good time when the conductor came up to me and said to see him after rehearsal. I was sure he was dropping me from the group for singing*

*flat or because my hair was too long or
something.*

*After the rehearsal he told me that he
had a friend who was doing some re-
cording and needed singers. That I wasn't
prepared for. For some reason, I never
called the number he gave me, and the
next Saturday I was getting high with my
friends again. I never made it back to
another Saturday rehearsal—I just
dropped out.*

—Harrison

In many ways, drug dependence outwardly resembles
the habitual-use stage of the addiction cycle, with no
one indicator that someone has crossed the line di-
viding one from the other. Users in both stages may
use daily and be preoccupied with their substances
of abuse; they often share the delusion that drug use
is somehow making life better; they usually don't
believe drugs are contributing to the problems crop-
ping up in all areas of their lives. The real difference
between dependence and habitual use is internal, and
it has more to do with why someone is using than
with how much they use or how often.

In the earlier stages of addiction a person is using a substance to feel *different*, to experience the effect they get from the drink or the drug. A person who
has reached drug dependence uses the substance to
feel *normal*. He or she wakes up feeling as if something is missing and can't wait until the first opportunity to use the substance again. Even when a depen-

dent person's intention is not to use—to stay clean for a while or stop altogether—he or she is powerless to stop without outside help. The drug-dependent user, or *addict*, no longer has the choice of whether or not to use.

Being dependent on a substance is much like an infant being dependent upon its mother. All attention and energy is focused in one place. When the addict's or infant's needs aren't met, there is discomfort and a feeling of emptiness and pain. Just as an infant cannot tell where he or she starts and the mother begins, the addict's substance is in control of the addict's feelings, thinking, and behavior—in short, his or her whole world. This helplessness, or what users describe as feeling "out of control," leads to lowered self-worth, or even self-hatred in drug-dependent persons.

There are many misconceptions about what being an addict is, even to those who are addicted. Intelligent, moral, caring, loving, considerate, talented, and attractive people become addicted. Drug dependence doesn't turn someone into a monster, but into someone who has no control over the urge to drink and use drugs. Users will focus on all the parts of their lives that still work so that they can say, "No way I'm an addict." This process of blocking awareness of drug use and its consequences is called denial.

Withdrawal and Substitution

One clear indication that a young person has become drug dependent is when he or she begins to experience symptoms of withdrawal, which are usually experienced as a very uncomfortable, "sick" feeling. Specific symptoms differ depending upon the substance and amount of regular use, though cravings for more of the drug are common to most users.

Danny recalls his first indication that his body was reacting to the need for heroin.

> I did a long run one weekend, just getting high around the clock for three days. That Monday I woke up sick, and I immediately knew that I needed more dope to make it stop. I think that was the first time it happened, because I had just been chippying a little bit before that, never shooting up every day.
>
> It's hard to communicate what it's like to be dope-sick to anybody who's never been there. It's about the lowest feeling in the world, like every joint in your body is aching while your stomach turns inside out. You want to crawl right out of your skin. No wonder kids'll do anything to get another fix. You'd sell your mother to a dealer to avoid that feeling.
>
> —Danny

Withdrawal is the result of cutting off, or "withdrawing," a particular substance after the body has become accustomed to a steady supply. When the amount in the bloodstream goes below a certain level, the body rebels. Hungover, the shakes, nic-fit, delirium tremens or DTs, dope-sick, and Jones-ing are all ways in which addicts describe their withdrawal symptoms.

Experiencing symptoms of withdrawal does not necessarily mean that a person has become drug dependent. A person who regularly uses medication for pain or sleep disturbance would experience withdrawal symptoms if the drugs were suddenly stopped, but those persons are not addicted. The difference is that their lives do not revolve around the use of those substances. They take medication to have more choices in life, not fewer.

The reverse is also true: Not all people who are drug dependent experience withdrawal. A weekend drinker, for example, may feel bad on Monday morning but can survive without a drink to get through the day. And many long-term marijuana users, while dependent upon a steady supply of pot, are remarkably free of physical symptoms when they "dry out" for an upcoming job interview or visit home.

Once someone has moved through this addiction process with one substance or addictive behavior, it becomes easier to develop dependence on another drug. The brain and body have already learned to respond to the introduction of a mood-altering chemical, so they have only to adapt to the new substance. This might explain why 60 percent of those who smoked marijuana before age fifteen later used cocaine, or why someone who smokes a pack of cigarettes a day before age seventeen is fifty times more likely to use heroin than someone who doesn't smoke.

Many young users, like Colette, substitute one substance for another, seeking to avoid the problems they associate with their old drug of choice.

I really loved it when I first started smoking pot, I just adored it. I was so funny, everything was hilarious, I laughed all the time. It was different than alcohol because you still had some awareness left. With alcohol, awareness got obliterated after a while. My brain got all fuzzy. I used to love doing both: drinking two beers, then getting high on pot. I started smoking only on weekends, but by the end of high school I was doing more pot because it was easier to get and cheaper in some ways. My boyfriend at the time loved to smoke pot, so we used to do it together.

—Colette

There are many reasons why a drug user at this stage may attempt to substitute another substance for his or her drug of choice. The user may have difficulty maintaining a supply or may believe that another substance will be an improvement. A young person who has a problem with alcohol may stop drinking and substitute smoking pot instead. It is very likely that he or she will become as dependent on smoking pot as on the alcohol.

When a user has reached the stage of drug dependence, getting free of an addictive substance becomes more than a simple matter of just quitting. From this point forward, getting drug free requires outside support and usually some form of treatment. Unless the drug-dependent person makes the commitment to stop and acts on it, the road to addiction leads to one of three places: a hospital, a jail, or a cemetery.

Stage 5: Life-Threatening Use

For Danny, using drugs was a long and strange journey that had passed through many dangerous places, but he had somehow managed to skate through each of them unharmed. When he finally came to the end of that journey, he was at risk for taking his own life.

> *I think I knew how bad it was, and that made me want to kill myself. Even shooting fifteen bags of heroin every day, I wasn't getting high. That just kept me from getting sick, and even that stopped working after a while.*
>
> *I drank at nights to try to get to sleep, smoked crack if I could find some, or stole Xanax off Dawn's mother to take the edge off. Nothing could stop the horrible way I felt. I thought my life was over.*
>
> *—Danny*

All stages of drug use carry a risk of bodily harm, either from the drug itself or the lifestyle that goes with it. Right from the experimentation stage, users risk overdosing from binge drinking or ingesting unknown substances. Obtaining drugs puts users into dangerous situations and places them at risk for assault or arrest. And when intoxicated, impaired judgment increases the risk of AIDS from unprotected sex or of making hasty decisions that could lead to homicide or suicide.

But in the final stage of the addiction process the user is faced with imminent and certain harm as a consequence of his or her drug dependence. One of three things can happen: The user's body breaks down due to drug-related illness; his or her mental state is impaired to the point at which the user considers suicide or neglects basic needs; or as a result of either drug-seeking or intoxication the user falls victim to accident or assault. All of these options are potentially fatal.

At the end of her addiction cycle, Nicole was at risk from sexually transmitted diseases, from accidental overdose, and from assault by the men she manipulated to obtain her drug of choice, cocaine.

At first, I refused to have sex with them. They all thought they were going to get some, but that's not the way it worked out. I'd just smoke up all the coke and then split. They would say all kinds of horrible things to me, but I didn't care. I'd already gotten what I wanted.

Once a guy caught me when I was trying to split. He was really pissed off about not having sex and he beat me up pretty bad. You'd think that would have scared me, but I was back in the bars two weeks later. I needed to get high, and I figured that was the only way I could afford it.

So I kept doing the same scam: Letting some guy at a bar get me drunk, pushing him to score some rock, then going off with him to use it. It got to where I didn't care if we had sex or not, as long as there was cocaine. The only thing that mattered was the buzz.

—Nicole

Depending upon what breaks down first, an addict at the life-threatening stage of addiction will either end up in a hospital for a physical condition, in treatment for a mental disorder, or in the criminal justice system through arrest. Sometimes everything falls apart at once, as when Danny was brought into the emergency room in police custody, referred to a psychiatric hospital for suicidal depression, but first had to be admitted to a medical unit because of pneumonia and dehydration.

At the end of her road to addiction, Colette was at risk to develop a serious mental disorder because of the effects of the drugs she was taking.

I was in a friend's house, and they had this thing where there were, like, eight bowls around this one pipe. We each got our own bowl of pot. So I smoked it, and I swear I blacked out, or I passed out. I don't know how long I was blacked out.

When I came to, I was, like, "Oh, my God, what just happened?" I couldn't talk the whole night, the fear was just so over-whelming. My leg was shaking—I couldn't stop tapping my foot, and I couldn't stop moving. It was very fright-ening, extremely scary. My friend's boy-friend said, "Colette, relax. Chill out or something."

I believe to this day that whatever was in the pipe was laced with something. I have never felt so extremely paranoid on pot any other time. And ever since then I've had panic attacks. Feelings of claus-trophobia come over me, my heart pounds, and I lose my hearing. I believe that whatever was in that pipe triggered it. And so I haven't smoked pot since be-cause it terrified me so much. So that ended that.

—Colette

Often there comes a moment when the addict real-izes that he or she has to stop. The problems that have been created by using are no longer able to be denied. This experience is referred to as *hitting bot-tom*. This is different for everyone, but it usually hap-pens when some outside consequence finally over-whelms the addict's ability to deny the problem. Al-though hitting bottom is usually brought on by some tragedy, it is a positive sign that he or she is ready to break the addictive process and reach for outside support. Everyone's bottom is different, and doesn't have to wait until the addict is at death's door. It can happen before the user has reached the stage of dependence, or at any point in the addiction process.

Whether the addict's "bottom" comes sooner or later has a lot to do with the attitude and actions of people around him or her. Many people respond to a friend or family member with a drug problem by trying to "help them out." They might lend the user money to obtain drugs or booze, ignore missed appointments or other inappropriate behavior, or hide drugs to keep him or her from getting busted. Instead of helping the addict to get better, the opposite is true: It takes longer for the user to hit bottom and seek help.

Separating an addict from the consequences of his or her behavior is called *enabling*. The more an addict is enabled to continue using, the longer it takes for him or her to hit bottom.

This was certainly the case for Danny, who was surrounded by well-meaning people whose behavior enabled him to sink deeper and deeper into his addictive behavior.

> *It was like everybody kept letting me off the hook. I stole from my grandmother, then from some of my mother's neighbors, I borrowed all kinds of money that I had no intention of paying back. The few times the cops picked me up, they would call Dawn's mother, who always came and bailed me out. Everyone would*

Co-dependent Relationships

The people closest to someone using drugs or alcohol often develop their own set of responses to the drinking or drugging. These survival mechanisms are sometimes called "co-dependence," and may actually keep the addict from getting the help they need. Answer these questions about your relationship with a drug or alcohol user as honestly as possible.

Have you ever...

1. called to give an excuse for someone who could not go to work or school because of too much "partying" the night before?
2. increased your own consumption of substances to keep up with someone who is using?
3. felt that it was a disgrace to talk about a drinking or drug problem?
4. cut down on outside activities so you could monitor someone's activity to keep them from using?
5. believed that if the friend or family member would just stop using drugs or drinking, everything would be okay?
6. thrown away alcohol or drugs to keep someone from using?
7. blamed yourself for someone's drinking or drugging?

If you are in a co-dependent relationship with a friend or family member, you need to learn how you can better help the addicted person.

*tell me I was a cute kid, I should
straighten up.*

*No one was willing to confront me un-
til it was too late. When people finally did
stop letting me get away with murder, I
took it out on them. It was, like, "How
come you're not letting me slide like you
used to?" By then I was breaking into
summer homes, passing hot checks, or
using anybody's credit card I could steal.
By the time I got locked up I had racked
up some major charges.*

—Danny

The healthiest attitude to have around an addict is to
give him or her back all the consequences of the
choice to use drugs or alcohol. What Danny needed
was not favors, but limits on his behavior. He might
have realized sooner that he was deeply in trouble if
those who loved him had made him accountable for
his actions. It may seem mean, or that it makes the
addicted person's life worse, but it is actually helping
to "raise their bottom." This is what the Al-Anon programs refer to as *tough love.* By not getting between
the addict and their bottom, it increases the chance
that he or she will get help sooner.

No one else is responsible for the losses the addict experiences as a result of drug or alcohol dependence. He or she is the only one who can make those
losses stop. When the user finally realizes that the road
to addiction leads to only one place, he or she is ready
to ask for help and begin the process of recovery.

RECOVERY

At the time, I really didn't want to. But going into treatment was the best thing that happened to me. Before that I was sleeping all the time, I didn't have a job, nothing to stop me from drinking. I got up one morning and started this program. My friend had given me a Big Book, so it just seemed the right time. I tried it for a day, then another day. I started to get a life. It was wonderful, miraculous.

—Colette

Recovery is more than getting straight, it is a chance for a new life. It gives a young person who has replaced the meaning in his or her life with drugs the opportunity to undo the damage done by these substances, and also to look deeply into what kind of life he or she wants to create. Just as addiction removes choice, recovery forces a young person to make choices about every part of his or her "new life," the one that starts when he or she gets clean and sober. It is a time of new thoughts, new feelings, and new behaviors. And this process, to be successful, lasts the rest of the former user's life.

Recovery does not have to wait until the drug user has lost everything or is at death's door. The process of recovery begins at whatever point he or she decides to get off the road to addiction. Treatment is available, and effective, at any point in the addiction cycle. During recovery the growth—emotional, developmental, relational—that was halted by the addiction process is allowed to continue. Because addiction affects every part of the addict's life, recovery involves healing on every level: the physical, mental, emotional, and spiritual.

Much like the road to addiction, recovery has its own stages through which the former user passes as he or she develops a clean and sober lifestyle. In this chapter we'll first explore how young people make the choice to engage in treatment, and how outside pressures can help in making that decision. We'll find out what kinds of support and treatment options are available in early recovery, as the recovering addict works toward physical safety while confronting addictive thinking. The middle stage will focus on the newly sober person connecting with his or her feelings and learning the behaviors necessary for living free of addictive substances. Finally, we'll explore the problems recovering addicts face as they reintegrate into the "real world" and enter long-term recovery.

Routes into Recovery

It was only with great reluctance that Colette was persuaded by her psychiatrist to enter addiction treatment.

> *I had stopped drinking on my own. I was able to stop drinking because my old boyfriend, who was my drinking buddy, had moved away. I was going to a psychiatrist, and he said, "Look, you have a problem with alcohol. Maybe I should send you to a program for addictions." And I said, "No, I just need a program for depression." He lied, and said, "They have no openings, so I'll have to send you to this addictions program instead."*
> —Colette

It is common for a young person using drugs or alcohol to realize that something is wrong. After losing a job, a girlfriend or boyfriend, or being thrown out of school, the user attempts to stop using on his or her own, resisting the idea that outside help is needed. Facing withdrawal alone, he or she frequently picks up the drink or drug again, or starts using another substance as a replacement. These failed attempts to get clean and sober only increase feelings of hopelessness and worthlessness, which isolate the drug user even further.

It is also common for those around the drug user to realize that there is a problem and to pressure that young person to enter recovery. Sometimes this takes the form of a planned confrontation, called an "intervention." The purpose of an intervention is to stop the addictive process by giving the addict back the consequences of his or her addictive behavior. This is also called "raising their bottom," because it confronts the addicted person's denial of the drinking or drug use before the situation gets worse. In a planned intervention, significant people in the user's life get together and try to communicate what effect the drinking or drug using has had on each of them. A counselor or therapist may be present to guide the session and offer treatment options if the user is ready. Some interventions are not planned, but result unexpectedly from a confrontation with parents, limits set by school, or by a run-in with the court system. For both Danny and Brandon, the choice of entering treatment rather than going to jail was a powerful motivator for getting into recovery.

When actively using, a drug user lives in the center of a private world. In order for recovery to begin, the user must let go of the fantasy that he or she is in control of the drinking or drug use. The longer the user resists surrendering this fantasy, the lower his or her bottom becomes, until eventually the choices are restricted to only two: stop using or die. A successful intervention can save the user's life by motivating him or her to engage in treatment and begin the process of recovery.

Stage I: Early Recovery

The first stage of recovery concentrates on restoring the user's physical safety and creating the support needed to help the addict carry through the entire process. A recovering person will need a great deal of support right from the beginning in the form of inpatient treatment and detoxification, daily twelve-step groups, counseling, and encouragement from friends and family to keep from falling back into old habits. As he or she is able to move further along the stages of recovery, the support system becomes an important part of reinforcing new behaviors and preventing relapse.

Colette needed the support she got from counselors in her treatment program to work through her denial about whether she had a problem with drugs and alcohol.

> *For the first week I kept saying, "I don't need this, I'm depressed." I still thought that I wasn't an alcoholic. I kept telling them, "I had a drinking problem but I quit on my own."*
>
> *We had to fill out some worksheets about our drug use and how it affected*

us, and some of the things I wrote started to sink in. I don't know what happened exactly, except I think my denial was worn down. I think it was the staff just being there, listening to me talk myself through it, being patient.

—Colette

People cannot act differently unless they think differently. At the very beginning of the recovery process, the addict's thinking needs to change about his or her relationship with substances, identify drinking and drugging as the problem, give up the fantasy that he or she can control drug use, and realize that support is available if he or she is willing to open up to it. At Narcotics Anonymous (NA) meetings members introduce themselves and say, "I'm an addict," to help other members know that they are not the only ones going through this. Starting these meetings very early in recovery helps to reinforce these changes in thinking, and to remind new members that others have made it successfully into recovery.

These new concepts are necessary for treatment to be successful, and hopefully they will continue throughout the recovering person's life. But no user is safe until his or her body is substance free.

Detoxification

The first task of treatment is for the drug user to attain *sobriety*. This drug-free state is both mental and physi-

(103)

cal. Sobriety allows the mind to clear and become free of the mistaken and self-defeating thoughts that held power over the thinking processes. Many of these beliefs began long before the addictive behavior; in fact, these mistaken beliefs are what compel young people to use drugs in the first place.

To attain sobriety, the toxic substances in the body must be removed. Once dependence has been reached, the substance needs to be gradually tapered out of the system. This process, called *detoxification*, or *detox*, may require medical supervision for a daily user to avoid dangerous withdrawal symptoms, especially seizures. Often, other medication is introduced to offset these symptoms or to make withdrawal more tolerable. The goal of detoxification is to get the user substance free, with one exception.

Narcotic addicts not ready to attempt sobriety can maintain their dependence on a legal and inexpensive supply of methadone. By switching their drug dependence from heroin, addicts can alter their lifestyles, avoiding the criminal behaviors formerly used to maintain their addiction, while engaging in some form of treatment. Methadone has a lower potential for abuse because of its timing: It acts much slower than heroin and other narcotics both entering and leaving the body. So addicts on a program of methadone maintenance can function rather normally while tapering off the drug over time.

After detoxification, the body gradually begins to adjust to a drug-free state. Treatment programs often incorporate daily routines for sleep, exercise, and nutrition so that the recovering person can learn to regulate these basic needs. Because all of the body's systems are adversely affected by addiction and the resultant neglect of the user's basic health, this process of repairing the damage can take many months—even years—to complete. Fortunately, young people have great resilience and can undo most of the physical damage of addiction while in recovery.

Treatment takes place in a variety of settings, including inpatient or outpatient hospital units, special adolescent treatment centers, doctors' or therapists' offices, and twelve-step and other self-help groups. Twelve-step groups like Narcotics Anonymous (NA) are based upon the steps for recovery and traditions developed by the fellowship of Alcoholics Anonymous (AA).

The treatment setting may change as the needs of the recovering person change, but will usually be more restrictive during detox and early recovery. The length of time necessary in each setting may vary due to a number of factors, but often starts with a short inpatient stay, transitions to outpatient groups or individual treatment for a longer period while new behaviors are learned, and later moves to twelve-step or other self-help groups for long-term recovery.

Because addiction is a "family disease," family work is an essential part of the treatment process. Just as in any situation where a family member is critically ill, addiction saps the resources of the whole family and puts a strain on every relationship in that family: not only between the addict and the other family members, but between other siblings and parents, and between the parents themselves.

The purpose of family counseling sessions and Al-Anon family groups, twelve-step programs for the other family members, is to heal every person in that family. Parents and other family members need to express their feelings of loss or betrayal without attacking the recovering drug user, and they need to learn how they can be helpful or harmful to the recovery process. Family members can contribute effectively to breaking down the user's denial and have an important place in the recovering person's support system. The more members of the family in recovery, the more likely that the entire family, including the addict, will reverse the negative effects of addictive behavior.

Stage II: Middle Recovery

At the point where the former user is out of physical danger and has a support system in place, middle recovery can begin. The recovering person is now safe enough to replace the habits that focused on drug use with new behaviors. These healthy habits—how to deal honestly with feelings and with others—will increase his or her ability to maintain sobriety and improve the overall quality of life.

For Michelle, who was ending a relationship with diet pills and crystal meth that began in her early teens, recovery brought the challenge of beginning a whole new life.

It's definitely better now, but I didn't feel that way at first. When I first stopped using speed, my world felt like it was coming apart. First the crash, like all the air had been sucked out of everything, mostly me. My body just refused to respond. Then the terrors that ran through my mind. I was fearful of people I knew, even more afraid of strangers. I thought the world was either out to keep me high or keep me from getting high, like there was some big plot against me from both sides. Then there were waves of boredom interspersed with periods of intense self-loathing, until gradually my head began to clear.

It has been a long, slow process, believe me. And it still takes all the courage I have to get out of bed in the morning. But at least I know it's me that gets to show up for life every day, not some drugged-out spook. It's hard sometimes, but it sure beats the alternative.

—Michelle

In this part of recovery, emotions that were "medicated" or ignored start surfacing, making middle recovery an emotional minefield. Young people in recovery have to deal with the insecurities and fears that they covered up as teenagers when they began using drugs. This can be frightening at first, especially when powerful emotions like fear or rage come flooding back.

It is natural for young people in recovery to be angry at those who promised them that drugs or alcohol would make their world a better place and fearful of those situations where they are at risk to start using drugs again. Other emotions get a recovering person in touch with needs and desires, and these feelings provide direction for how to act as well as the motivation to meet those needs. Emotions like fear and anger are essential in avoiding danger, and they assist the recovering person in keeping safe and sober.

Raymond did a lot of things when he was high on inhalants that he now regrets. Now in recovery, he is learning to deal honestly with all of his feelings, even the difficult ones.

> *I did a lot of things when I was sniffing and drinking that I regret now. I was really mean to my girlfriend's kids and did some other things I'd rather not talk about. I'm really a nice guy, but it wasn't me when I was getting high. I was a bastard.*
>
> *I go to church now, I go to AA. You don't feel so alone when you belong some-*

where. After years of trying to hide from everyone, I am able to be straight with people. Most of all, I don't lie to myself anymore. That's what sobriety's about.

—Raymond

Because addiction erodes a young person's ability to be truthful, the most important new behavior learned in recovery is being truthful with oneself and with others. It is also very important for the recovering person to take responsibility for the damage caused by his or her addictive behavior: physical, financial, and criminal.

Relapse

There is a risk at this stage for the recovering person to be overcome by the demands of the future and the wreckage of the past. To a person who has used substances addictively, the most natural response to being overwhelmed is to reach for a drink or a drug. This slip back into addictive thinking and behavior is called a *relapse*. A good support system is the best prevention for a relapse, which is why support is necessary at every stage of recovery.

There are many ways in which recovering addicts set themselves up to fail, but the most common have to do with falling back to old ways of thinking. Recovering addicts may believe that they can control the substance or that they can stay straight without help or that recovery is different for them than for anyone else. This is what members of AA have dubbed "stinkin' thinkin'." When this happens, the newly recovered person begins using drugs again and usually winds up at the very same stage of the addiction process where he or she left off. Sometimes it takes many tries before a young person can stay straight. But recovery is available at any point on the road to addiction.

The process of recovery is difficult, but it has rewards. At the very least, each day in recovery brings another day without drinking or drugs. But it also brings back the possibility of regaining physical and emotional health, as Colette discovered a few weeks after entering a treatment program.

Since I stopped drinking, all my health problems have cleared up, except for my asthma. It's just a miraculous recovery, like overnight, from quitting smoking and quitting drinking.

And then there are the kids I used to party with who are still drinking every night and partying, looking older and older and out of place. It's horrible.

—*Colette*

Those who have been challenged by addiction are often motivated to work on developing a healthy lifestyle. They are able to incorporate new behaviors based on the knowledge gained in early recovery by listening to feelings and needs without the mask of drugs and alcohol. When they can feel their feelings,

(110)

are comfortable with these new behaviors, and have a support system firmly in place, they are ready for the next stage of recovery.

Stage III: Long-term Recovery

Recovery, like life, is definitely a struggle. There are good days and bad days, and not every risk pays off. This "real world" is not portrayed for us in ads or on TV where everyone is cool, no one is seriously challenged except by what clothes to wear, and every problem reaches a simple solution in either thirty or sixty minutes, minus the commercials. But there is something joyous, even exciting, about the daily challenge of the real world.

The final stage of recovery is about "getting a life," about getting back to sanity after the craziness of drinking and drug use. After crawling back from the nightmare of his addiction, and with a great deal of support, Danny has finally reached the real world.

I never thought this day would come. I wake up now and wonder what I'm gonna do today. That's very different from waking up and looking for the bag I stashed last night so I can shoot up, then wondering how I'm gonna get the money to go cop some more. When I was using, a day meant nothing more than dragging myself from fix to fix. Now each day is the first day of the rest of my life, just like they say.

(111)

Nothing's certain. I worry about all the same things everybody else does. I heard somebody at an NA meeting talk about "process, not perfection" and I'm beginning to realize what that means. Now that I'm clean, I get a chance to make my life better every single day. And life is getting better—one day at a time.

—Danny

Recovery is more than just getting off drugs or alcohol. It's about getting in touch with reality, and learning to live it, accept it, and grow from it. One of the attractions of addiction for young people is the simplicity it gives their lives, the certainty that every day will be reduced to only one challenge—maintaining the supply and avoiding withdrawal. Getting straight is about adding more choices to life, about finding lots of ways to deal with all the unpredictable changes that life throws at every one of us, and learning to handle all of these challenges with feeling, with honesty, and with some style.

When he reached this stage of recovery, Raymond found out that he had a great deal of rebuilding to do to create a life for himself.

I had a lot to catch up on. When I started getting high, I was doing poorly in school, and had barely learned to read. I got sober and realized that if I was going to make it in this world, I had to finish high school, and that meant starting right from the beginning. Luckily, I had some wonderful teachers who helped me get my G.E.D. And a lot of support from the other people I met at my meetings. Some days, it felt like everyone I knew was rooting for me to make it. That was nothing like when I was getting high. Back then I thought that no one cared at all.

—Raymond

A recovering person must sometimes face the damage that addiction has done to relationships and to his or her goals for the future. Raymond was forced to accept that he had missed out on learning to read because of his addiction to inhalants and alcohol. His reckless and violent behavior when intoxicated had caused harm to others. In recovery, he is now able to try to compensate for the pain he has caused himself and others.

Colette also has some regrets about the choices she made while using pot and alcohol, and the fact that her life, when compared to her age mates, seems to have some pieces missing.

It's still real hard for me to believe I'm an alcoholic 'cause I'm still young. Other people who haven't gone through what I have are starting to get through college,

settle down in careers or families, do
something with their lives. They have a
focus. I feel like I really missed out when
I was drinking 'cause my only focus was
partying and going out.
    So that's part of my recovery, dealing
with that. I believe now that I am capable
of finding out where my life is going, and
I can be grateful that I've been given this
chance to get straight and figure it out.

    —Colette

An important task of long-term recovery is continuing to build and strengthen support. By building positive relationships with others at work and play, the recovering person turns every part of his or her community into a network of sober support. This relationship between a healthy person and a healthy community helps build a new sense of self, one that connects with the outside world both socially and spiritually, and allows the recovering person to start living a life that focuses both on meeting his or her own needs and giving back and helping others.

    Colette has been able to find meaning in the influence she has on other young people just entering recovery.

So now I'm active in the AA program. I'm
helping people now, especially young
people. They said this in the meeting:
That just by my being in these meetings,

(114)

that if a young person walks in and sees me, that's really good for me and for them. Because then they know that they're not the only young person who is dealing with this.

—*Colette*

In long-term recovery, the recovering person engages in the struggle—and the possibility of triumph—that comes with facing the world without the limitations that drugs and other addictive behaviors provide. He or she attempts to integrate changes in lifestyle and friends and learns new ways of relating to others that don't rely on getting high. These changes, taken one day at a time, gradually build into a whole new life.

addict: a person dependent upon some mood-altering chemical or behavior. Not every *substance abuser* is an addict.

addiction: a dependence upon some mood-altering chemical or behavior, often with life-threatening consequences.

binge: an intentional rapid intoxication of five or more drinks in a single sitting.

blackout: a level of intoxication resulting in no memory of events afterward.

controlled substance: an illicit drug whose possession and sale are prohibited by law. Also called *hard drugs.*

denial: the process of blocking awareness of drug use and its consequences.

depressants: substances that sedate, or put to sleep, the central nervous system. They include alcohol, anti-anxiety medications such as Valium and Xanax, barbiturates such as Seconal, and many of the inhalants.

designer drugs: chemicals manufactured in home labs to imitate controlled substances, usually stimulants or hallucinogens.

(117)

detoxification or *detox:* the process of safely withdrawing a toxic or an addictive substance from the body, or a facility where this process takes place.

drug dependence: a pathological relationship with a mood-altering chemical or behavior.

gateway drugs: the substances used by those first experimenting with substances—tobacco, alcohol, and marijuana—whose continued abuse strongly predicts whether a user will "graduate" to other illegal substances. Also referred to as *soft drugs.*

hallucinations: Altered perceptions of reality, usually involving seeing or hearing things that aren't there or are vastly different from what is perceived by others. These are sometimes terrifying.

hallucinogens: substances that induce an altered state, including distorted perceptions of time, space, and the user's physical limitations; dramatic mood changes; intensified feelings; and *hallucinations.*

hitting bottom: the point at which the consequences of addictive behavior breaks through to the user's awareness.

inhalants: substances found in household and industrial products that are inhaled for the purpose of intoxication. These include solvents, aerosol products, and anesthetics.

intoxication: a reduced state of brain functioning caused by poisoning the body with a toxic substance.

minimization: attempts to lessen the seriousness and importance of addictive or substance-abusive behavior.

narcotic analgesics: drugs that work on the central nervous system to block messages that come from pain receptors; also called *opiates.*

over the counter: medications available legally from a pharmacy that have a potential for abuse.

overdose: a potentially lethal ingestion of a substance,

(118)

usually resulting in one or more of the body's systems shutting down.

potency: the ability of a drug to produce an effect, usually an unknown quantity in drugs obtained illegally.

purity: the presence or absence of contaminants in a substance, also an unknown quantity in drugs obtained illegally.

recovery: the process of reversing dependence upon or abuse of an addictive substance or behavior.

self-esteem: appreciation of one's own value, individuality, and rights, particularly in relationships with others.

self-help group: a form of *treatment* for a variety of problems that relies on the support and wisdom of others recovering from the same disease. Most common in addiction treatment are twelve-step groups.

stimulants: drugs that increase the activity of neurotransmitters, increasing alertness and energy, while blocking sensations of appetite and fatigue.

substance abuse: the use of addictive drugs or alcohol with potentially life-threatening consequences. Not every substance abuser is *drug dependent.*

tolerance: after the body has become accustomed to a particular substance, more is required to produce the same effect.

treatment: any of a number of therapeutic options to reverse the effects of addiction or substance abuse. Most common are hospital-based, outpatient, and *self-help groups.*

twelve-step group: a *self-help group* based upon the steps for *recovery* and traditions developed by the fellowship of Alcoholics Anonymous (AA).

withdrawal: the symptoms of bodily discomfort or distress in a *drug dependent* person when the amount of the addictive substance in the bloodstream goes below a certain level.

Sources for Help and Information

This is a list of phone numbers and addresses for national hotlines that provide information ab out addiction and referrals for addiction treatment. Also check the community service numbers in the front of any NYNEX phone directory for addiction services in your area. They are usually listed under the heading "Alcohol."

AIDS HOTLINE
1-800-342-2437

AL-ANON FAMILY GROUP WORLD SERVICES
P.O. Box 862, Midtown Station
New York, NY 10018-0862
Phone: 212-302-7240

ALCOHOL AND DRUG COUNSELING HOTLINE
1-800-ALCOHOL

ALCOHOLICS ANONYMOUS WORLD SERVICES
P.O. Box 459
Grand Central Station
New York, NY 10163
Phone: 212-686-1100

AMERICAN CANCER SOCIETY
Atlanta, GA
1-800-227-2345

AMERICAN LUNG ASSOCIATION
1740 Broadway
New York, NY 10019-4374
Phone: 212-315-8700

MOTHERS AGAINST DRUNK DRIVING
Phone: 1-800-633-6233

NATIONAL COCAINE HOTLINE
1-800-COCAINE

Methcathinone (CAT), 60, 61
Mexican Americans, 53
Middle recovery, 106-111
Monitoring the Future survey, 10, 56
Moral judgment, 67
Morphine, 65
Mothers Against Drunk Driving, 122
Motor vehicle accidents, 46

Narcotic analgesics, 65-68
Narcotics Anonymous (NA), 103, 105
National Cocaine Hotline, 122
National Council on Alcoholism, 45
Native Americans, 53
Neurotransmitters, 60
Nicotine, 21, 42-45
Nitrous oxide, 52

Opiates, 65
Opium, 65
Overachievers, 30-32
Overdose, accidental, 9, 10, 39, 41, 68

Pain medications, 54, 65
Paint thinners, 46, 52
Panic attacks, 94
Paranoia, 63, 94
Parental substance abuse, 28-30

PCP, 64
Peer pressure, 17, 18, 70
Percocet, 65
Planned intervention, 101-102
Pleasure center of brain, 65
Pornography, 21
Potency, 40
Pot (*see* Marijuana)
Power hitting, 25
Pregnancy, 46, 81
Prescription medication, 41, 42, 54, 55, 65
Prostitution, 61, 67

"Raising their bottom," 101
Recovery, 11-12, 91, 98-115
  early, 102-106
  intervention, 101-102
  long-term, 111-115
  middle, 106-111
  relapse, 109-111
  routes into, 100-102
Relapse, 109-111
Rescuer stereotype, 30-32
Risk taking, 21
Ritalin, 42
Rohypnol (roofies), 46-48
"Roid rages," 51
Role models, 28-30, 50

Scapegoat stereotype, 32-33
Seconal, 42, 46

(126)